The Hamlet Secret

A Self-Directed (Shakespearean) Workbook for Living a Passionate, Joy-Filled Life

James M. Lynch

authorHOUSE®

AuthorHouse™
1663 Liberty Drive
Bloomington, IN 47403
www.authorhouse.com
Phone: 1-800-839-8640

First published by AuthorHouse 6/29/2009

ISBN: 978-1-4389-6066-1 (sc)

Printed in the United States of America
Bloomington, Indiana

This book is printed on acid-free paper.

Dedication and thanks go to:

My weekly angels, who called and asked if I did what I said I would do and never "sold me out": Rosie and Cliff

The people who created the Mission Impossible course with me and who had the courage to take on their lives with me:

Bill, Derrick, Mike, Patricia

Special thanks to Anna.

Thank you and love to Riv, who gave me the "space" to write this.

He (Shakespeare) was the man of all modern, and perhaps ancient poets, had the largest and most comprehensive soul ... He was naturally learned; he needed not the spectacles of books to read nature; he looked inwards, and found her there.

John Dryden

Introduction

Several years ago I was an actor in a one-man workshop called **The Hamlet Secret** that was conceived by doctoral candidate Naum Panovsky, now a prominent theatre director in Macedonia, in a program led by the gifted Professor Victor Turner. The dean of the department was the amazing genius Robert W. Corrigan, and I look back at this period of my life with awe for the learning, friendship, and creative fertility I was able to enjoy. As I learned my lines (and some of the other characters' as it was a one-man show) I heard many of the lines of the world's most famous play as if for the first time. On that bare, deconstructed set, I realized the power of "there is nothing, either good or bad, but thinking makes it so" and "to thine own self be true."

In the following years I became more and more involved in the world of personal transformation, personal growth, contexts and distinctions, personal coaching, and business/executive consulting, but the truths of this play, *the most performed, written about, and widely read play in the history of the world*, never left me. In fact they've served me well. Many years later I am ready to share this work with you, and my hope is that it moves you forward in your goals and your pursuit of your life's purpose.

This work is touched upon in my seminar series, **Being the Star of Your Own Life**, which applies the lessons of acting to living the life of your dreams with power and authenticity. Find out more at *www.starofyourownlife.com*.

About the Author

—James M. Lynch has had several careers in the first half of his life, including theater, business, consulting, personal coaching, and development. His business consulting focuses on small(er) businesses and creating a working culture of passion and energy. He has a background in most of the major transformational technologies, including having been executive director for an Illinois-based leadership and personal development program, and he leads seminars, Being the Star of Your Own Life, that include a lot of the material in this book. He lives in a north shore suburb of Chicago with his amazingly wonderful wife and three fun, funny, loving, and creative children. He is also a visual artist, creating undisciplined canvases and natural art installations and promoting arts in his community.

For more information see the afterword—"Transforming the Author"

How to use this book

You can read from cover to cover if you'd like, but don't read too fast; take the time to do the exercises and to let the lessons in.

> Or
>
> Randomly open the book and read what you find. If it doesn't provide an immediate answer, just keep it in your head for a week or so and watch what happens.
>
> Or
>
> Leave it on a bench in a park with a "read me" note attached with instructions for the next person who reads it to do the same.
>
> Or
>
> Buy extra copies and share them with friends to create a "Hamlet Secret Society."

Challenge—If you're not sure if this book is for you, then open it to a random chapter. Read the lesson and copy down the exercise. Do the exercise for one week as instructed, and at the end of the week ask yourself: is this making a difference in my life? If the answer is "yes" and you're ready to dive deeper into a passionate, joy-filled life, then come back, buy the book, and get to work. Better yet, buy several copies of the book as I suggest above (Hamlet Secret Society), give them to friends and family, and invite them along on the journey of self-discovery. Do the same chapters at the same times, or each pick a different one and compare results in a weekly group meeting. The support of others is great but not necessary; this book is designed to give results whether or not your involve others. Just don't spend too much time "thinking about it" or you risk losing "the name of action."

The readiness is all!

Bernardo: Who's there?
Francisco: Nay, answer *me*. Stand and unfold *yourself*.

Hamlet, Act I, Scene 1

The reference here is to two guards meeting each other in the dark and each demanding the other to identify himself. It's dark and cold, and they are wrapped up in cloaks against the cold so they need to ask: *unfold yourself.*

So, here's your chance to unfold YOUR "self."

What is the "cloak" you've wrapped around your true self that keeps people around you from recognizing you—not just in the dark, but in the plain light of day?

Give yourself some credit, first of all: you're here; you're reading this. That means on some level, even if you are experiencing fear, reluctance, or skepticism, you are up to something.

You have begun, or are continuing, to unfold.

Let's start our exercises with this one on the following page: "unfold *your* self."

Unfold Yourself Exercise:

Write your name: _____Age: _____ Weight: _____

    (Before we go any further: any problem writing down your true age and weight? If the answer is "yes," do this pre-exercise: find a full-length mirror and stand in front of it. Say your name, true age, and true weight over and over again until it becomes just a fact with no "interpretations" (like *good or bad, fat or bony, old or immature*). Your goal is just to "get it" about *what's so*. You'll have plenty of chances to take yourself on in the coming chapters, so don't worry about doing it all at once, ok?)

What does everyone know about you?

(Occupation, family, clubs/organizations, financial situation, etc.)

What do only a few of your closest friends know about you?

What does only one other person in the world know about you?

What do you hide from the world?

Describe yourself as if you were writing a bio for the back leaf of a book you wrote (under one hundred fifty words but no less than fifty). Spend some time on this one and make it crisp and clear. This is selling "you," so keep it positive and upbeat.

Bonus: Take out your resume, if you have one, and bring it up to date. If it seems disjointed or out of touch with your career goals, go online and read some articles on creating a better resume and apply the tools. If you don't have a professional resume or don't work or have a work history, then write a personal resume of the "chunks" of your life: Hobbies, Favorite Movies, Professions I'd like to have, Education, etc.

Journal time:

Now take out your personal journal (or take the time to get one if you don't already have one) and write down ways you're already aware of that you hide your true self from others. Every day for a week write down times that you noticed when you held back from saying what you truly wanted to say, when you were not your true self or weren't 100 percent honest with yourself or others.

NOTE: This is just writing a list or capturing an event. It is not about solving a problem or beating yourself up for being a phony or a fake, for example. Just write what happened and what you might have wanted to have happened differently, or what could have happened differently. We're building skills here, so be ok with keeping it simple, ok?

When this is complete, you're done and you can go on to the next chapter. Really. We're just getting started here, and it can be a lot of work just to get to "what's so"; don't try to over-analyze or make too much of this.

If there be any good thing to be done that may to thee do ease and grace to me, speak to me.

Hamlet, Act I, Scene 1

One of the best ways to get what you want is to just come right out and ask for it.

So let's say you are ready to break up with your lover because he or she is not "floating your boat." This person "fits" in social, family, hobby, and other ways and is otherwise a great match, but is not physically "delivering," for instance, or some other pedestrian want or need is not being met. Well here's a radical idea for you: DID YOU EVER THINK OF TELLING HIM OR HER WHAT YOU WANT? Thinking that the other person "should know without asking" is such a childish, selfish and unproductive way of behaving that I want to reach out and shake you if you say it! Give people a chance to live up to *and* into what you need without having to develop their ESP to the point where they can read your mind.

Do you know what might also work? Asking and having him or her say "no." We often assume a "no" ahead of time, so why not risk it and ask: win or lose, but get done with it. Doesn't it seem a more courageous way to live?

The *dark side* of this not asking is the "being right" virus. By keeping inside all that you want from others you get to be right about the fact that they won't or can't deliver, and you get to avoid actually facing life head on. If you did ask and did "receive," you'd have to let go of a part of the myth you've created about life. HINT: this is exactly where you want to go!

This Hamlet scene mentioned in this quote, by the way, is between a guard and a ghost: it takes a lot of courage to take on a specter and say, "Just tell me what you want"! Could you imagine trying it with a LIVE person? Hmmm, sounds like time for another exercise.

Speak to Them Exercises:

Exercise 1:

Make one *outrageous request* per day. Choose from the suggestions below or go from your own list. Don't get attached to getting a "yes" or a "no"; just see what happens and be warned that *you may just get what you want.* Then what will you do? Be prepared to accept the responsibility that goes with living full-out.

Sample Outrageous Requests:

At work, ask for a promotion, an earlier-than-expected raise, more vacation time, or paid medical insurance. Request extra paid time off to take a self-improvement course or to start a community service initiative. Ask your boss to assign a mentor to speed up your career development or something else you've been holding off asking about. If you know what you want, set up a meeting with the appropriate people, think your idea through beforehand, and make a clear, well-spoken request.

At home, ask your spouse/partner/kids to share more of the household tasks. Set aside a "safe talk" time and talk to your lover about intimate behaviors you've been too shy or reluctant to discuss. Call your banker and ask for few interest-free months on your home equity loan as you "financially regroup." Ask for a no-penalty month off from a mortgage payment. Ask for late fees or overdraft fees to be reduced, relaxed, or eliminated. Ask for an hour more on Sunday mornings to sleep in.

With friends, set up time to discuss what makes you crazy about them and ask permission to be really honest with them when it happens. *"You always show up late with some excuse. How about we make an agreement to be on time no matter what with each other and cut out the excuses?"*

In public, ask someone in the checkout line if you can cut in front of him or her because you have an urgent appointment. This is an exercise, and—I don't believe I'm saying this—you don't really have to be late for an urgent appointment; you're just trying it out (stop and give the person a candy bar or something if he or she says "yes").

A primer to help you get started: "If you knew that every day you could make one request that no one could say 'no' to, that there'd be no repercussions for, what would that one request be?"

2. The list:

Write a list of everything in life that bugs you, then think about who you could ask for help with those things. For instance, you don't want to keep doing Thanksgiving dinner at your parents' house when your own home has more room, a bigger kitchen, and is more centrally located. You could call your mother or father, tell him or her what you're thinking, and ask for support in bringing it up to the rest of the family. Put about five or six things on the list and an "ally" for each and begin living in the possibility that you just might get what you want. Then start making the calls!

The magic statement:

For some reason, if you start your outrageous request with the statement, "*This may seem like an outrageous request ...*" people seem to want to say "yes" just to prove you wrong or out of a desire to help. Try it!

All that lives must die, passing through nature to eternity.

Hamlet, Act I, Scene 2

Life is short—*what are you doing about it?*

"Passing through nature to eternity ..." Whether you believe in the afterlife in any of its many forms—heaven, rebirth, hell, and purgatory—you might believe in the laws of physics; energy can neither be created nor destroyed. So what becomes of this life force once we "shuffle off this mortal coil"?

Believe anything you want about life, but right here and now, today, and in this present "act," **choose the life you have** *and get on with it.* Recently I heard it said that in relative terms of scientific discovery and breakthroughs, it is possible that the first human to live to be two hundred years old could already have been born. BUT he or she will still die sometime, and what happens between the cradle and the grave is a daily choice we must make in order to make it all worth it.

Start living from "today's the day" and taking on everything in life that you've been avoiding—either do it or cross it off your list forever. No time for regrets, anger, or fear, unless you like that sort of thing. I mean, no one really LIKES that sort of stuff, do they? Then why would they fill their lives with it? Got me? Perhaps this will help before we get to the exercises: **What you do** *today* **is what your life will become tomorrow**. That ought to get you moving, eh?

All that lives must die exercises:

Exercise 1:

For one week, do at least one thing a day that is new or that scares you, even just a little bit. For example, I am not knowledgeable about baseball, but I had a chance to coach third base for an inning in my son's little league team. I said "yes," even though I was unsure of what to do. The third runner I signaled home was my own son, and seeing him poised on second base was the high point of my day! Journal each night about what you did and your reaction to it.

Exercise 2:

> This one you probably saw coming: write your obituary as if you died today. Tell the truth and don't make anything up. AND you can't add anything that might have happened if you could have lived.
>
> Now, go ahead and give yourself another five years; now what would your obit say? Ten years? Twenty? Then get about doing the actions that you need to make your obituary read like you want it to. Don't get fooled that you have one more moment in life than this moment now, or you may just get lazy again!
>
> The last part of this exercise is to rip up all the obits into little bits and throw them away. We don't want that kind of energy hanging around us, do we?

Exercise 3:

Take a sheet of paper and draw a line down the center: label the left side "committed to" and the right side "showing up in my space." On the left side write down all the things you are committed to having in your life or that you intended to have in your life by now (like owning a house, having kids, how much money you'd have, your physical state, etc.). On the right side of the page write down what is actually showing up in your life, what is true. Now take your two labels and *switch them*. What is showing up in your life will now be labeled "committed to." What is showing up in your life now, what is true in your life now, is what you're *actually committed to*. If you weren't committed to it, how would it be showing up in your life? Did someone else put it there? You just have to let that sink in for a little bit before you can do anything about it. See, you can't buy a ticket to anywhere without first knowing where you ARE now.

"I'd like a ticket to Tahiti, please."

"Certainly. What airport will you be leaving from?"

"Does it matter?"

"Well, yeah!"

"Seems? I know not 'seems'... They are actions that a man might play. I have that within which passes show."

Hamlet, Act I, Scene 2

Be authentic.

In my former life as an actor, acting teacher, and director and working with actors I was aware of how much DRAMA they surround their lives with—I mean, no kidding, eh? But it's true about a lot of us that we create a drama bigger than what is actually going on.

We get caught up in something other than the fact of what is happening and over-indulge in our emotions. Clean it up, and you will notice how much clearer your life becomes. Take the time to create awareness around each emotion you encounter. Remove the "coping" that comes with all of the difficult scenarios and deal "soberly" with life. I choose "sober" here because we have so many crutches, not the least favorite being drugs or alcohol, but anything that comes up as a way to deal with the difficult situations, from that holiday meal with family to parties with people you don't know well or like too much. Spend a moment and do an inventory of what is "driving you" in these situations. Do you need a smoke, need a drink, feel self-conscious about what you're wearing, or not want to attend at the last moment? These are signs that you are addicted to the "actions that a man might play." The real "juice" is in getting in touch with that "within which passes show," the what-is-going-on in your life, triggered by something that happened long ago and that is still running you like a puppet.

Create an awareness of the reactions that occur so automatically that you might have stopped noticing them.

13

Seems Exercise:

This is a BIG exercise and complex but very powerful, so don't put it off. Today's the day, remember?

On the left hand side of a page in your journal make a single-row list of all of your "crutches." Don't be afraid—I haven't asked you to give any of them up; just make the list. Start with the ones that you know are a reaction to stress, circumstances, or other influences. The big ones are easy, like smoking, drinking, nail biting, overeating, illicit drugs, legal drugs (like valium), sex (solo or promiscuous behavior), etc. Keep extending the list to the less obvious crutches. The smaller ones might take a little more thought like staying up late, watching a lot of TV, shopping/buying, irritability/yelling, lateness, distraction at work, procrastination, etc.

Now take a highlighter and mark the items that will undoubtedly shorten your life, like smoking. Get help from a doctor, counselor, professional program, etc. on those dangerous items and don't wait to "figure them out." By the time you figure them out you may be dead. Tough love time, guys: it won't work. Get help; be responsible.

For the next MONTH, to the right of the habit, write down how many times it occurred in that day. Try to associate each of the habits with a "trigger" or just plain old where it occurred.

Now add one column to this list, on the far right—"Rank for today/ rank for life in general today." (Score this 1 through 10, with "10" being life is GREAT)

After a few days, but at least by the second week, start looking for a pattern in the list: the example could look like this:

"Cigarettes—39—all day and including at Tina's party, today was a 6/ life overall 8"

In our sample we'd see that the days leading up to this one you usually smoked twenty-five cigarettes or fewer. Did you smoke more on this day because you were at the party, or because it was just a "6"? Check to

14

see if any of your other "habits" varied in intensity for this day and try to check out what it was that was causing the variance. Was the party the "trigger"? Was it something about the party—not a lot of people you knew, etc.?

We're not really taking on the behaviors in this exercise; we're just cataloguing them with the aim of creating AWARENESS for all the hidden "drivers" that are controlling us. They may still control us after this exercise, but we'll be aware of the choice we're making (nobody's perfect) and we'll be consciously choosing—that's big!

Note: We're looking to identify your triggers, and not just the "big ticket" items but all of them. We want the awareness while the event is about to occur, is just occurring, or while we're already deep, deep, IN it! For example, I quit a lot of my worst behaviors and then noticed that for one stretch of time, like a week or so, I was staying up way too late watching TV and paying for it the next morning. I always thought staying up late watching TV was just something I enjoyed, a holdover from adolescence and not a reaction to any outside events in my life. I was wrong. Now, when I catch myself staying up late I "go backwards" and ask myself, "What is going on in my life that I'm reacting to, and why am I not taking it on or being authentic about it?" Or, I'll say, "I'm going to stay up late tonight—I need to be a little self-indulgent right now." No guilt. I'm choosing; I'm a human being, and I need some crutches to live. In the long run I'd rather lose a little sleep than smoke a cigarette or drink or drug myself into a so-called "safe place." It is an opportunity to know myself a little better!

You must know your father lost a father;
that father lost, lost his; and the survivor
bound in filial obligation for some term to
do obsequious sorrow. But to persevere in
obstinate condolement is a course of impious
stubbornness. It shows a will most incorrect
to heaven.

Hamlet, Act I, Scene 2

Don't hold on to grief too long; it becomes a "back door" you use to escape the joy and pain of living your own life.

The Jewish tradition of grieving is very structured: for seven days you are totally indulgent. Immediate family members in mourning don't wash, don't take care of their appearance; people come and take care of their needs, and for that whole week they are as self-indulgent as they can be—it's expected. Then for a year they recite a short prayer every day and then honor the memory of the deceased every year on the anniversary of his or her passing. In this way you get to "go into" your sadness but not so far that you can't get out of it again. You get to say goodbye and then get back into living with no disrespect for the memory of the departed.

Remember, grief and sadness over a loved one *is not about him or her*, or anyone else for that matter; it is about *you*. It is an intense emotion, an "emotional high" though technically labeled a "low," but it is just as intoxicating as a drug or liquor. Use of this intoxicant can lead to abuse, and to dwell on this sadness is to "thumb your nose" at all of the living going on around you: it is incorrect to heaven.

Grief Exercise:

This one is simple, yet not easy. You could do it in a journal, but it's best to write this on loose sheets of paper.

Write a letter:

> to someone you love who is deceased, or
> prematurely to a living parent "as if" he or she were deceased, or
> to someone in your life who is chronically not well

The letter should be a farewell letter that you would feel comfortable reading in front of the person.

Now write the letter from your "dark side" and let out every fear, anger, and "pissed off" particle of your body. If you don't feel it, embellish and pretend; be a drama queen and really self-indulge.

Write the letter again as if it was all a really great story someone told you—"The story of a parent who ...," "My dead ... ," "The incredible sickness of ..." Use the perspective of a distanced observer telling the story in a book of fiction.

Write the letter one more time using a combination of all of the above and using all you've learned about yourself in the process.

Tear up all versions of the letter.

If the person you were writing to has passed away, do something nice to commemorate his or her life like making a donation in his or her honor or bringing flowers to his or her grave. If you wrote your letter to your still living parent(s), send him or her (or them) a small "thinking of you" card or something similar. If your letter was to someone who is chronically ill, send him or her a little note or bring him or her a small gift.

Move on with YOUR living and enjoy your life as fully as possible, realizing that it is all you, all your choice, and all of your making.

Need more help? Contact me, and I'll help get you a reading list.

Foul deeds will rise, though all the earth overwhelm them, to men's eyes.

Hamlet, Act I, Scene 2

There's no use trying to sweep dirt under the rug …

People will inevitably find out about your "hidden sin," and it could happen just when you want it the least. *Les Miserables* is Victor Hugo's story of Jean Val Jean, a poor man who steals a loaf of bread (the candlesticks come later) to feed his family and is caught and punished for the crime. As the story goes, he escapes prison and makes up many times over for any wrong he might have done. Over the many years of his life in seeming freedom he is forced to twice deal with this past coming back to him in the guise of an inflexibly righteous bulldog of a policeman named Javert. Lots of lessons for all, but in the end Val Jean and Javert both need to give their lives in order to free themselves of the pain of their consciences. Could Val Jean and Javert be "the miserable ones" of the title because they are laboring under a foul deed that has accumulated more weight with each year, one neither of them has been able to let go of for his individual reasons?

Yes, there IS a little voice in the back of your head that reminds you of all the stupid and mean things you've done, and it will remind you to the point of making you crazy. That is, it will make you crazy until you take it on, get it over with, say you're sorry, and offer an apology. I know that you ask forgiveness; I don't know if you need to get it! Just admitting it out loud, saying "I was wrong," is like lifting a weight off your back.

Now this doesn't in any way sound like fun, and who the heck would intentionally take on something that they might feel guilty about but that they "got away with"—well, the answer is YOU would. Instead of treating this as your punishment, you could take the approach of "mining" the situation for the freedom and clarity it might offer. Here you are, walking around with a "sin" or some other "foul deed" on your soul that gives you more and more proof of how intrinsically and irreparably "bad" you are. In truth, you don't even know if what happened was what *really* happened, if what you remember was *actually true*, or if the person you wronged even remembers or cares.

At any rate, you get to clear your soul, be true to yourself, and indulge that side of yourself that is you without any of the "accumulations" we weigh ourselves down with. Go after your ills, real or imagined, say "I was wrong," and begin to fly a little freer.

Foul Deeds exercise:

Write a "sorry" letter and include everyone you've ever wronged, everything you've ever done that you feel guilty about, and any other "guilt" you're carrying. If there is something you're guiltily enjoying, like you stole money from someone, give it up or give it back if possible. If it's not possible, make a gift to charity in that amount or as much as you can safely give. On this list of things, if any of them can be undone, go ahead and undo them, but NOT at the expense of your family and friends who have moved on from it. You may need help deciding which is which on this one, so get help from a coach, a minister/priest/rabbi, or some other trusted advisor and face the fear.

At the very least, when you're finished this list, take it out somewhere safe and burn it. Say out loud, "I forgive myself for the sins of the past and will work to create a better life in the future," and mean it. Don't forget: we're human, and we make mistakes. We can often be weak and frail and sometimes very, very selfish. Don't use this fact to step on others, but don't use it to beat yourself up and punish yourself. Make the best choice you can in the present moment and move on!

Virtue itself escapes not calumnious strokes.
Hamlet, Act I, Scene 3

Be careful of envy…

… especially when it comes out as "smack talk." How often do you hear people denigrate a really great achievement or accomplishment?

It starts with someone praising someone else upon hearing a report of a particular achievement or accomplishment. Then a comment shoots out that begins with "Yeah, but …," and the rest of the comment goes on to explain how the achievement or accomplishment was really a result of luck, inheritance, gift, or some other "excuse" that deflates the honor. I know you've heard this before and—why is that?

Let's say it belongs to *jealousy*, first and foremost, but let's not overlook the fear that really fuels it. A temptation to denigrate anyone else's achievement is to put further distance between ourselves and the achievement we ourselves can reach. If we can discount someone else's accomplishment, we can excuse either our own lack of accomplishment or numb/dull the passion and drive we naturally own. Let's look at someone who just won a local mayoral race and say, "Good for him (or her)," rather than, "Well, he (or she) is wealthy and connected to all the 'money people' in town."

Encourage and applaud others for the results they show. See the result for what they are—often a compilation of luck, hard work, circumstance, fate and a "touch of G-d." There is nothing to be envied as much as appreciated, and the comparison of them to you is only valuable if it inspires you to "get in the game" and go for your dreams.

Applaud the greatness in those around you; the favor will be returned if you do.

Exercise for Calumny:

Listen for incidents of calumny. You'll know an incident is imminent when you hear a sentence that starts with: "Yeah, but he/she/they …"

Do NOT indulge yourself. If someone around you begins to excuse or dismiss someone else's accomplishments, keep out of it. You may think I'd encourage stepping in or calling other people on it, but really, let's take the approach of not adding fuel to the fire as opposed to being the "Calumny Cop" in your own social circle.

Journal what it is that you would do, that you would accomplish, that represents you at your best, your highest, and your high point of your life. Keep that energy alive however you might choose (we'll have exercises to choose from) and make that dream happen sooner than later.

This is an admittedly clumsy and sideways means to go about it, but think about it: what is in your means to accomplish that would cause others would talk about you with the phrase, "Yeah, but he/she/they …"

Get that "thick skin" on against any comments that pull you back and keep you down; don't allow the words to get into your head.

Listen to the cheers when they come, the support that's there every day, and the "source voice" that keeps moving you back to the REAL you, the YOU under all the layers you've added since childhood.

Do not, as some ungracious pastors do, show me the steep and thorny way to heaven whiles like a puffed and reckless libertine himself the primrose path of dalliance treads and recks not his own rede.

Hamlet, Act I, Scene 3

Don't give advice unless you're also willing to live by it. For years now politicians have been depicted as two-faced liars espousing "family values" while keeping mistresses or gay lovers stashed away somewhere. The "watchdogs" of society, I am afraid, really believed that they had a duty to tell everyone the right way to live even if they themselves were not able to. The term "leader" has become a tainted badge at best.

Don't give up on being a leader, but do lead from example rather than empty rhetoric. Creating ideals, by definition impossible to attain, that aren't coupled with reality will destroy more lives and spirits than any good the "steep and thorny way" might produce.

Acknowledge your fears, your foibles, your own missteps along the way, and don't preach from too far above the crowd—it makes it harder to hear you.

Reck your own reed Exercise:

Get a band-aid. I recommend a colorful one so that it will catch your attention.

Put it on the end of your dominant hand's forefinger and wear it for three to five days. For example, if you're right handed, put it on your right forefinger.

The band-aid is there to help you notice any time you point your finger at anyone else, saying, "You should …" or any time you give advice or instruction. This includes sending the kids to bed early when you yourself don't get a full eight hours sleep a night.

Journal all the times you notice yourself giving advice or saying "you should" to anyone else. Notice if you keep your own advice, and listen to yourself while you're talking to others. If it's good for them, why not you?

This one is fairly simple and can give you some gentle insights, so don't overdo it. Just "notice and journal" for at least three days, ok?

Give every man thy ear, but few thy voice.
Hamlet, Act I, Scene 3

Listen more than you talk.

In sales training there is a ratio of success in listening: seventy/thirty. Your "prospect" should be doing 70 percent of the talking; you get the other 30 percent. Old-fashioned sales models were about "convincing" while the more modern model is to listen to what the client has to say and address only that—don't oversell or talk too much. That is why, they say, we have twice as many ears as mouths.

You have an opportunity to allow every human being you encounter to contribute to you in some way; all you have to do is listen to him or her with care and respect. Something he or she says will move you forward. Listening TO what someone is saying is way different from listening FOR an opportunity to chime in, to turn the conversation back to you, to debate, to build your point on someone else's platform. Listening to someone is the greatest gift you can give. Give it often, as it pays dividends.

The quote actually means something a little slyer than what I've said above, as its original intention was that you should withhold saying what's on your mind. The variation on this that works for me is that you should take time to listen, to weigh what you hear, and only to share what you're thinking (heaven forbid you share what you KNOW— that's like an intellectual dead end) with someone that you trust. Then a conversation can come up, a back-and-forth can take place, and you'll feel sharing from the heart.

Save the 30 percent when you'll talk until you have something really urgent to share from your heart about something that is occurring right in the moment, and say it when it can be heard and to someone who will listen.

Few Thy Voice Exercise:

This is another band-aid exercise. Remember that bright, colorful, or fun (borrow from your kids) band-aids work best.

Put one band-aid on the little knuckles of each hand (pinkies).

All day long as you talk to anyone use the band-aids as a reminder to stop talking about you—stop talking at all—and to ask about the other person in the conversation. Notice how many times in the day you're talking versus listening.

Your goal for the day will be to learn something new, something not obvious, or something surprising about the people you interact with, from the server who pours your coffee to the person who shares your office.

Journal what it feels like to begin really *listening*. This one is a "starter project." It takes years of practice, and I recommend a communications course before you can really learn to listen effectively. But get started today and learn "on the job."

Neither a borrower nor a lender be, for the loan oft loses both itself and friend.
Hamlet, Act I, Scene 3

Never lend more than you can afford to lose nor borrow what you can't pay back.

Don't take this one wrong here; it is ok to ask for help. Consider the myth of men who won't ask for directions but who would rather drive around NOT getting where they are going. I say "myth" as it isn't fair to men who are ok with allowing others to contribute to them, allowing that they don't know it all and that it means nothing to be in someone's debt.

DO take this on face value if you are at all tempted to use someone else's money to live beyond your means. Credit is an extension until you can pay the money back and should be used wisely. The current trend is to live on debt without a real plan to pay it back. It leaves you vulnerable in a way that could spell worse consequences than NOT having now and having to wait for the reward (scary thought, eh?)

As far as being a "lender," it is ok to give wisely as a means to support someone else's goals or to help a temporary situation. Unfortunately, "throwing good after bad" is more often than not the situation, and someone who is afraid to lose his or her business, let's say, might have already done so but is afraid to face the consequence. Are you being a true friend by buying someone time? You could be selling out on the truth instead.

If you do lend money, do it generously and with pride in the ability to say "yes" when asked. NEVER give from any place other than empowerment or consider yourself superior for being able to give.

Lender Exercise:

This is not so much an exercise as a practice, but it will, if you'll pardon the pun, pay off.

Pick your easiest-to-pay-off recurring bill or credit card. Budget your other payments so that you can pay extra on this one account and pay it off sooner. Once it's paid off, add that same amount of dollars to the bill with the next-lowest amount. Once that one is paid off, keep paying the same amount as both of them to the next account, and so on and so forth. Before you know it you'll be paying off your extended credit and be able to live debt-free.

I know this sounds VERY simplistic and naïve, especially if you have some hefty amount of debt out there, but you just need to get started now and stay the course. It works on paper, so why not use it in life?

If your debt is worse than that, get help from a financial advisor or find other resources that are available to help you recover from out-of-control debt.

If this is not your issue and your finances are fine, all the better. There's other work to do.

To thine own self be true, and it must follow, as the night the day, thou canst not then be false to any man.

Hamlet, Act I, Scene 3

If you keep integrity with yourself first, you will keep it with others.

Ok, now how do I write anything about this one: "to thine own self be true"? I mean, it just makes sense, right? I'll just do what I want and not worry about the consequence because it's all about **me**, baby, and if I hold back my desires, if I don't "just do it" then I'm not living up to my full potential. Live fast, die young, and leave a good-looking corpse. To MY own self be true! It's all about the instant gratification, and all we have is now, now, now. Yippeeeekaaaaaaaaaiiiiiiiiiiiiooooooooooo!

Well, now let's consider to thine own "TRUE" self be true. Let's go back to that child who you WERE before you became the victim of consequence and conditions. Let's visit the "you" before you decided what it took to survive. Not hard, you say—you have always been the same person? That makes this harder to tell you, but... NO, you're not YOU. You are someone you made up to survive the crap being dumped on you and in order to avoid EVER getting hurt like that again. And you've repeated that pattern again and again and again every time you faced the same situation to the point that you've built up an emotional callus, a virtual numbness that can't be overcome by reading one single book, taking one single class, or doing ten sessions with the hottest life coach. As people say about Shakespeare, there are only thirty-five to thirty-seven plots, and every story written before or after Shakespeare can be reduced to one of them (boy meets girl, boy loses girl, for example).

You need to do the work, take a course, do a meditation, and I can't give it all to you in one chapter—this isn't THAT book. But since we're here I'll give a little explanation and a brief suggestion to get you through.

As I said, we started reacting to life and finding a way to deal with pain—"that which does not kill us makes us stronger" according to Mr. Nietsche. But, dear Friedrich, may I ask: "stronger" in what way and at what expense? If as a young child we are hurt by the death of a family member we might feel such extreme pain that we make a decision never to hurt that badly again. Quite possibly, the best way we can avoid ever feeling that much loss again is never to care that much again.

We will no longer be as vulnerable; we will hold a piece of ourselves in reserve. So the next time we feel ourselves beginning to love, that survival mechanism kicks in and we follow the pattern we've created. Then something not exactly the same, but similar, say the chance to have something we really, really want to have, comes along. But this time we're afraid we won't get what we want and then we'll feel deep loss in the way the original "hurt" felt, so we apply the same logic and pretend not to care if we get what we want or not. We hold back, we pull back, we create this safety without realizing that this is really just locking our true self away, piece by piece.

By the time we're say, eighteen or nineteen, we've faced many good/bad experiences, exercised our safety mechanisms so often that we're pretty safe to go out into the "real world." But our TRUE self, now skilled at avoiding "hurt," is partially anesthetized, bound and gagged in the back room for its own good. We wind up living out our entire lives with the rules created between the ages of six and eighteen. What chance do we have with a child's emotional rules in place? That's why so many of us behave like children!

TRUE SELF exercise:

This is not enough to countermand years and years of numbness conditioning—but it is a start.

Create a list of the "perfect" person and what the perfect person, if it WERE you, would look like. Suspend all disbelief and write the fiction of you as you could be if money, time, opinion, doubt, "common sense," and those parts of you that say "get real" were removed.

Now list the person you would be, the things you would do daily and regularly if you were the person you don't presently think you could be.

Next take one thing off this list, one thing this person does, and put it into your life for real. If for example it is "get up and go for a bike ride every morning," then add something physical to your life—maybe not every morning, maybe you don't own a bike or can't afford one. The details don't matter; the action does.

Debriefing this exercise: It's important to get into action to be a little closer, right now, to the true self you've been denying for so long. Shake off the shackles of protection, safety, and reserve just one link at a time. Return, with the true wisdom of an adult, to the realm of "everything is possible" and question everything in order to recreate the "rules of the road" as a conscious, aware, adult.

Don't forget to honor and thank the child who kept you relatively safe and who guarded your pain for so long. Wish him or her well—you'll see that child again and again, but take the reins back; it's time. And to your own *true self* be true.

.

When the blood burns, how prodigal the soul lends the tongue vows.

Hamlet, Act I, Scene 3

Beware of promises made in the heat of the moment.

Our minds are in control, and our minds like order, safety, reliability, repetition, pattern, and predictability. Thank goodness for their liking these things because we rely on our mind to do some pretty mundane tasks about a million times a day, like breathe, pump blood, regulate our heartbeat, heal, restructure and renew, think and possibly "feel"; after all, we know our hearts don't really "feel," so it has to be from your mind, right?

In Shakespeare's time, and for a long while before and after, it was thought that our emotions were kept in our differing and various organs. The spleen was the keeper of anger—as a matter of fact we still describe a person with a hot temper (a metaphor with its own interesting origin) as "splenitive." It's a bit of a digression from the point, I guess, and I don't have a rational explanation of why I went there just now but *I just felt like it.*

Get me? I mean, how often do you say you'll do something and then call and cancel, with or without an excuse or reason, when the truth of the matter is you just plain old didn't feel like it? I planned to sit down and write ten pages of my book tonight, but it was a long day, the kids were difficult, I needed to rest my mind, and "I just didn't feel like it." Well boo-friggin-hoo, for you and your "feelings"; if you don't take this one on and get it handled, you will find yourself disappointing yourself and others more and more and more!

If you make a promise, do it. If you give your word, keep it. No excuses, no reason, no "I-don't-feel-like-it." Grow up and grow into the person who keeps your word in the face of challenges, low energy, barometric pressure, someone else giving you a "pass on this one," and all the other everyday, normal, and expected and excusable ways we get around living up to our words. Yes, others are implicated too, because for most people we don't even care, we don't even expect people to live up to their words, so they in turn don't expect us to live up to our words either as a kind of professional courtesy.

But there are those bastards out there messing up this dirty little double standard and keeping their word. You should hate these people because they're going to raise the bar, ruin the "curve" and make it harder for the rest of us to slough off our promises. They will deliver on their word whether they feel like it or not, and pretty soon they'll be living incredible, powerful, effective lives and making the rest of us look bad.

Uh, oh, here's one of those "the old way isn't good enough any more" types now—holding this book!

Psst, don't worry; it's ok. It's not easy, and you don't have to beat yourself up about it. It's like any muscle you need to develop. Start small and build up to it. The more times you flex it, the more powerful it becomes. You'll blow it a lot at first, less more and more as you go, and you will still, at all levels, still not FEEL like it sometimes, but that's the beauty of it. You don't have to be a victim to your feelings, and if you work through it the "not today" feelings just sort of push off. Take your time—work your way up to it and flex the muscle until it's strong. I won't tell anyone about you and this new strength—I'll leave it up to you to show the world.

And if you get this one piece of this puzzle, be assured, the world WILL know.

Good luck to you.

Tongue Vows Exercise:

For the next week carry a stone in your pocket. Not so big that your pants will fall down, but big enough that you'll be aware of it.

The stone is to remind you to be 'present' to your word as you give it and, more importantly, for the times when you want to break it. For the next week, no matter what comes up, keep your appointments, follow through on your commitments, and do everything on your calendar or to-do list. Journal about your experience of yourself as you live this rigorous life of your word.

By the way, if your friends try to cancel an appointment on you, invite them to keep the meeting, make the meeting earlier or later, but do your best to do everything you said you'd do. If FEELS great, by the way, if things like *feelings* count for you.

Meet it is I set it down that one may smile, and smile, and be a villain.

Hamlet, Act I, Scene 4

Remember that a smile sometimes hides sharp teeth.

So now let's talk about you and how you are a villain. WHAT, ME? Yes, YOU. How do you do it? Why, you smile and smile and hide your true purpose. You do it subtly and masterfully, as the greatest of all antagonists from any play, and you can even fool yourself. You may say "yes" and mean "no."

Please stop reading for a moment: we need to talk. When you read the quotation, I bet you thought I'd get all righteous about "bad" people, didn't you? There's enough of them around, and we spend not just a little of our time judging them, don't we? We keep thinking that if they changed, or weren't in our lives, or just "got it," or if we could just set them straight, then it would all be ok and your life would be easier, right? We blame them for a lot.

So here's why I am going in this particular direction right now: spending any time trying to change anyone else is a complete waste of time until you take YOU on. Not only that, blaming anyone else for what's going on in your life is not only insincere, it is giving away your power and makes you small and weak. Don't go there, ok? I'm glad we had this talk; let's continue.

Let's use a generic situation you may know personally or at least can identify with in order to get this one out. Let's say you have a boss, and the boss makes a decision, creates a plan, or gives you an assignment. In your mind it's stupid, wrong, or he or she should have let YOU handle it. But you smile, and maybe you argue a little for your point, but probably because he or she is stupid and wrong, your boss doesn't see your point. So you agree, at least you say you do, and then go out to enact the plan or fill in others as to what the decision is.

As you're not 100 percent on board with the idea, every time you talk about it you remarks are either tinged with complaint or you introduce it as a faulty or a stupid idea. You give the impression that it is an idea that you are forced to act on, or you just plain don't take appropriate action, and the idea, plan, project, etc. falls on its face. You win. You smiled and sabotaged. You were so intent on being right, even at the cost of others' money, time, reputation, etc., that you "said" yes and then behaved as a "no." Getting what they want, at the expense of others, regardless of the consequence so that they get to fulfill an ego desire is what villains do, isn't it? Some come out and declare it. Be honest about being a villain if you're intent on behaving like one.

You may have been subtle about it and just conveyed your criticism with a shrug of the shoulders, a roll of your eyes, a harrumph in your throat, or a tone of voice, and that is somewhat worse; it is sneaky and can be habit forming. In none of these actions is there courage, direction, or power. In none of these does the positive energy that you want to create and manifest get expressed. You have become a saboteur, a villain.

Now, your situation may not be as obvious or dire as this one. It may not be as much on the surface or apparent even to you. You may be the boss, or you may be doing it to a spouse, a parent, sibling, or anyone in your life, but we all need to look at ourselves and check that our smile isn't hiding our "villain-self."

"Examples gross as earth exhort me," but I don't want to make this too long. Please just take a look at times when you say one thing and mean another. It may not be with a smile; it may be the best you can do—in fact I believe it is the best we THINK we can do in all cases—but it still needs looking into. Don't be smug, don't consider yourself above it, and don't think you know exactly whom I am writing about—unless you think I'm writing about YOU (and me, too).

I know of at least one quick way to deal with this, so let me briefly offer a solution. If you are involved in a decision or plan and you disagree, then speak up. Ask questions, argue fact, argue opinion (carefully labeling each one as it is: "I feel" or "I think" as opposed to "We all know it to be true ...") Be as clear as you can and try to truly listen with an open mind to the responses, facts, and opinions spoken in reply, being aware that there is always more than one way to do most anything.

If at the end of the process you still don't agree or just plain old run out of time, try for *alignment*—agreeing to go with the plan in spite of your opposition. Often alignment is the only path when many are involved. Alignment is only possible if your voice was heard, you held nothing back, and you act from a position of respecting those around you. Respecting them is up to you, too; a common misconception is that others have to EARN your respect—NOPE! If there is true alignment, then you can go out and give 100 percent, be truly supportive, and learn to be in relationship with others who are NOT you. If it doesn't happen all at once, give it some effort. If you find yourself always out of agreement, always out of alignment, and in short supply of respect, then it's time to see a coach and make some changes. You may need a change of venue to find your way back to the place you were meant to be. "Or not to be …"

Villain Exercise:

First I ask that you re-read the entry again in the next few days to let it truly sink in. The behaviors I'm discussing are very subtle and subconscious and may have become so habitual that we'll need to peel the many layers of the onion slowly.

The "exercise" is more of a practice and is without end. In brief it is this: carry a pad and pen into all meetings. When a supervisor or project leader makes a request or announces a procedure, write down *exactly* what he or she is asking of you. Read back the instruction or request and make sure that *what you heard* was *what he or she said.* If you have questions, ask them now.

The next step is to enact your part in the process to the letter of the instruction as you wrote it down. If there is a problem or a roadblock, go back to the others involved and let them know what you're facing. Take action based on the actual agreement or instruction, and not your version of it.

When *giving* instruction, ask the person you are assigning to perform the task to write down what you're asking, and then have him or her read it back to you. Get clear, get specific, get related, and most of all, get used to it. You *don't* know it all, by the way, and letting someone else be "boss" can be a great growing experience.

There are more things in heaven and earth, Horatio, than are dreamt of in your philosophy.

Hamlet, Act I, Scene 5

Don't let what you know get in the way of what you can learn.

At face value this can be about the existence of UFOs, ghosts, Big Foot, or heaven and/or hell; it could be our discussion, and that might be enough. However, this is not that book. You're on your own with that particular avenue of discourse if you choose to pursue it.

What I am using this particular Hamlet quote for is for those of you who are ready to create yourselves anew. This is about trust and surrender. Recently I was leading a course on creating the impossible—results that would be considered impossible, improbable, unlikely, or on the "I've always wanted to" list. Two participants argued that their goals didn't fit into the model I was suggesting. One participant was re-thinking his end result before actually delivering on his scheduling, planning, and statement (three initial components of the course).

Their arguments and "push back" were perfect and expected—I had actually planned for their push back; in fact I was counting on it to drive the night's discussion. They were, of course, applying their strengths— that is, what had worked for them in the past (or "not worked" in a sense)—to an assignment that didn't require it. In fact, they were trying to "think" through something that required no thought. Thinking is limited, of course, to your brain power, and your brain, whether you're Einstein or a simpleton, is no match for the universe or G-d.

Mastery in life calls for prayer, meditation, and openness to the lessons of the universe, truly being able to get out of the way of the instruction that is coming to you and acceptance on a level that even the most excellent of "brains" can't comprehend. We need to learn to listen with our hearts and decide with our "guts." That is where mastery of life comes from.

Your Philosophy Exercise:

Make a list of all the things you've accomplished in the last six months. Next to each one of them, write down the short-version "story" of how they were accomplished.

Who helped you complete them in any way?

What got in your way that you had to deal with, and how did you deal with it?

Did any of your accomplishments rely on "luck"?

Did you get any "lucky breaks"?

Rank them on the scale of "hard" (10) to "easy" (1).

Now make a list of the same size (as many items as above) of things you will commit to accomplishing in the next six months. *For the purpose of this exercise assume that all things are possible.*

Next, write the story of how you will accomplish those things with the premise that the first part of the exercise has given you an indication of "how things work.'"

For example, in order to accomplish this new list:

Who will you need to ask for help?

What could possibly get in your way, and how could you plan ahead to avoid this obstacle or what needs to get put in place now so that you can handle it later?

Remember Thomas Jefferson's quote: "I am a great believer in luck, and I find the harder I work, the more I have of it." Schedule the "hard work" in your calendar that will bring you your luck.

What would a "lucky break" look like in accomplishing this? How can you arrange a "lucky break"?

Rank these future accomplishments in order of difficulty in accomplishing them, 10 being really challenging, 1 being "easy to accomplish."

Now all you have to do is accomplish all the things on your list. You may want to start with the "easy to accomplish" items so that you build up to the more challenging items, but the important part of all of this is to make things happen because you said they would happen. Planning on asking for help and planning out the "luck" you will get will change your definition of "luck" and show you just how things REALLY work.

The time is out of joint. O, cursed spite, that ever I was born to set it right.

Hamlet, Act I, Scene V

Take responsibility for change in the world.

Mahatma K. Gandhi said, "You must be the change you wish to see in world," and there is no more damning indictment in the world. In this scene Hamlet gets it that he's been hiding from life, from the truth, from the responsibility of action, and he's been called on it. It's a play, by the way, and you may not get a chance for your dead father the king to come back as a ghost and kick you into action. Instead you could move to "*The Land of 100 Percent Responsibility.*" Here's how to get there.

The *Land of 100 Percent Responsibility* is a made-up world; it's not true, it's not real, and you will argue with me, unless you get it, that it is a place to "come from" or be but not a literal occurrence.

Simply stated: it is all YOU, no matter what. Whatever the result, whatever happened, it is *all your "fault"* (read "*responsibility*"). By adopting this stance, you become empowered to take on any situation no matter what. Let's say you ask someone to bring home milk, eggs, and flour and he or she forgets, even though you wrote the list down and stuck it in his or her pocket. You have the option of being upset, blaming the person, reinforcing whatever negative opinion you have of him or her (gathering evidence is always GREAT) or taking 100 percent responsibility for the event. In the non-make believe world you are right that you took appropriate action if you say, Well, I wrote it down and stuck it in his (or her) pocket and he (or she) still screwed it up." You would have the right to be disappointed—but you would still be out of milk, eggs, and flour. Taking 100 percent responsibility gives you the chance to consider how this could have happened and how you can assure that in the future you'll get what you need, when you need it, with as much of a guarantee as is possible in this world.

Consider this: when you are driving down the road and someone pulls ahead of you and into your lane, cutting you off, and you have an accident, the other driver is clearly to blame. But you BOTH have dents in your car, right?

Out of Joint Exercise:

Do this writing exercise in your journal. Take a simple breakdown that has occurred lately to *The Land of 100 Percent Responsibility* and, no matter how far you have to reach, figure out how *you yourself caused it*. See if you can find a solution you previously didn't think possible. Be super creative and, remember, this is not a reality-based exercise (though the solutions I've come up with using this seem to be very practical and real). If you do this a few times you may, like Hamlet, see that you have been choosing to bury your head in the sand and not seeing what needs doing. You may be "bearing those ills" instead of *being in appropriate action*.

The time is "out of joint," and it is up to you to set it right. And the time will always be "out of joint" even though the world is just perfect as it is, as there is something for you to care about and care for: people, places, or things. It is time for you to consider the Jewish "tikkun olam" principle of "healing the world" as each and every individual's task here on earth.

And don't forget that taking 100 percent responsibility for your life is a happy task, one that gives joy, returns more energy to you than what you expend. It is a key to happiness in this life, and this is the only life we know for sure, isn't it?

Brevity is the soul of wit.
Hamlet, Act II, Scene 2

Keep it simple, stupid. (KISS)

I'm damned before I start writing about this one—it contains its own instruction, doesn't it? Well, here goes: the answer to every question is "yes" or "no." That's it. Anything that follows the word "because" is a lie. A thing either is, or it is not. Got it? Take a moment to read those few words over again and just let the ideas play around in your head a bit. Don't "think" or labor about them, just let them in to roam around that great big melon of yours.

Did you really take time, or are you rushing through life again? It's up to you; I can wait if you want to take more time. No? Ok. At the risk of betraying the phrase by expanding on it, there is a parallel to get to the truth in its simplest form. In the "sales" game, whenever I had a team to coach out of a slump, the hardest lesson I could ever get the team to accept, and the first one I took on, was to get their answers to "yes" or "no" without a long story of explanation.

We would have our initial meetings where we would commit to actions and then agree to a check-in meeting in the next few days. When we'd get to the check-in meetings I would ask them if they had indeed done what they committed to doing. It was fairly predictable, unless they'd worked with me before or had actually done all they committed to, that all of them would launch into a litany of all the reasons and excuses why they didn't do what they said they would do.

Again and again I would stop them and say, "Take the whole idea of 'good/bad,' 'right/wrong' out of it and just say 'yes, I did it' or 'no, I didn't.'" It would take a while, but once we actually got to the simple facts, then we could move forward at lightning speed. You can't imagine the face of someone who finally gets free of the fog of excuses and reasons.

Once we'd gotten this straight, "yes and no" conversation, then could we recognize, let alone take on, the many distractions that had been more important than keeping their word. To be truly free and in the flow of a passionate life, whatever gets in the way of you keeping your word needs to be exposed. Get free, baby!

Maybe a definition of "integrity" will help here. First, what integrity is not: it is not a moral stance from where you get to judge someone else. It is not "truth." Integrity is simply doing what you said you would do by when you said you would do it.

If you don't do what you said by when you said, then you are out of integrity. Now what do you do? You "fess up" to not doing what you said by when you said you would, make a sincere (that's a crucial consideration) re-commitment, and then you follow through. If you don't deliver the next time, if it's other than a "yes, I did," then it is time to re-look at what you were saying you'd do and whether you actually have the intention of doing it or not—really. REALLY.

One other important part of the definition of integrity is that what you say you'll do has to be big enough. It is easy to commit to doing something simple, something small, and then give yourself plenty of time to do it. How you can really use integrity as a power tool for growth and development is by getting in the habit of committing to things outside of your comfort zone, that are a stretch and that involve a certain amount of risk. Then integrity becomes a tool, not a place of self-satisfaction (which is the first step on the path to complacency, smugness, and an out-of-control ego).

Brevity Exercise:

Start on Sunday night. Make a list of things that you'll do this week. It doesn't have to be a complex list; as a matter of fact *simple* is best: four or five things at most, and they can come off your "to do" list as long as they're not too predictable (e.g., walk the dog, pick up laundry, etc.).

Now divide these tasks up over the week and decide the days that you'll do them. If possible, invite someone into the exercises for you to be accountable to. Give that person the list of things and the day you said they'd be done. Ask him or her to check in with you on that day and simply ask, "Did you do it?" Your goal is to answer with a simple "yes" or "no." No guilt, no excuse, no drama.

Try it for a second week and a third and just notice how your relationship with your promises begins to shift. Once you've mastered it—and I mean REALLY done this, not just predicted the outcome and done the exercise in a virtual reality—then journal about what it opened up for you. Thank the person who held you accountable with a little gift, and if you didn't involve someone else but just wrote in your book—why? Get others involved, and you may just open a door. Ok?

More matter with less art.
Hamlet, Act II, Scene 2

Be direct.

The shortest distance between two points is a straight line, and the shortest route to "connectedness" is a straight conversation. After many years of managing others, especially having to conduct reviews, remedial conversations, and dismissals, I had to master "straight talk." What I realized was that the truth, delivered with care and respect, was the key. The realization for all of us to have is that when we sugar-coat our words or beat around the bush, we are doing it for our own sake. If you have any awareness at all you realize that this kind of communication doesn't feel good and leaves you with a kind of "intellectual film" or residue.

How can you take the situation and reduce it to the "matter"? Well, first of all, what is expected? What has been communicated that is not being delivered? If it is something like telling people that they've been taking lunches that are too long, have you ever told them how long they CAN take for lunch? How many times and how clearly? Are you being "subtle" or unclear or expecting people to read your mind?

You should never enter a dismissal conversation with an employee or a break-up conversation with a lover in which he or she is at all surprised or not expecting it. It is your job to say, realistically, plainly, in as few words as possible, what you expect, by when, and then review the results. Do your best, especially if this is a work environment, to keep your personal morals and judgment out of it and refer to behaviors, undelivered expectations, and facts.

How do you know that you're getting it right? Try this: at the end of any remedial conversation or feedback session with someone, ask:

"Do you feel that this conversation was conducted with respect?"
"Could you repeat back to me what you got from it?"

Then see if *what you said* is *what the person heard*. If not, you have more work to do.

When do you really know you've got it? When you dismiss an employee and he or she thanks you for it and walks away with pride and a sense of a new beginning. And it's not easy!

More Matter Exercise:

For the next week, commit to saying what you want in as few words as possible.

Start simple, with the dry cleaners, the valet, a co-worker, your spouse, or mate. Tell the person what you really want in as few words as possible.

For example, at the dry cleaners, you might say, "Your machine has been flattening my shirt collars. I want them to stand up crisply on their own as I don't wear ties often." This happened to me; they gave me an assurance, then crushed the collar, then told us that there was nothing to do about it as this machine just worked that way. We switched dry cleaners—no muss, no fuss.

With a co-worker, pick something that would help in creating more passion or more concentrated effort at your workplace. What is interfering or interrupting you? Ask co-workers to give you "focus time" for an hour or two each day where no one can interrupt, when you don't answer e-mails, when your phone is on "do not disturb." You may have to negotiate this with your supervisor, but if you frame it in a desire to increase production and be more effective, you should have an easier time of it.

With your spouse or mate/partner: "I want you to help with the (cooking, cleaning, make beds, etc.) at least (once/twice/three times weekly)" or something that you've begun to see as a burden. Pick something that is less weighted than "quit smoking" or "lose twenty pounds," etc., as this is an exercise and just practice. Those are important things, yes, but this is about changes YOU are up to.

Now *the key to ALL of these is that you OWN both the request and the response.* The request has to be made clearly, respectfully, at the right time, without prejudice, and with no "weight" of accusation involved. If your request involves a sore spot or ongoing unspoken resentment for you, then diffuse it first or don't use it. The response, whether a "yes" or a "no," is just a response and has no meaning. It is what happens when you are direct, and people aren't used to that, so give them a little "space." If you got a "no," walk away from it a while and consider if it's that important or if you're being stubborn. Let it go or re-enter into negotiations later, once you've had a chance to breathe a thousand breaths.

People may not like your directness at first, and you may make some mistakes; it's new. Take time to ask people, "Is it ok that I'm direct?" "Do you mind if I'm blunt?" "Was it ok the way I asked you for this?" Get feedback from people and you can take responsibility for how your words "land." THAT'S A HUGE PIECE TO GET!

To be honest, as this world goes, is to be one man picked out of ten thousand.

Hamlet, Act II, Scene 2

Be that one person.

I looked up the word "honest" and am mystified that if it is so simply being "good or true" then how come so much is written about it? And why are there so many synonyms and ways to describe what it *isn't*? And why are most of the definitions of "honest" tied into moral, ethical ("Honestly, Confucius and Socrates will talk your ears off!") and "good" when a person can say, "I'm going to cheat, steal and rob" and still be "honest"? It's all good and worthwhile reading, and I'll leave you to it, but please don't ask me to wait this time—you may never come back from that rabbit hole.

Let's just have it that if you say so, it becomes so, and leave it at that. Admittedly it's not easy to do and in reality, it is probably fewer than one person picked out of ten thousand who is actually honest in doing as they say. We are so used to people spouting absolute cow dung that we don't even notice the stink anymore, do we? We lose power, and so do they, because we waste our dreams on talk, complaint, "what if," "why not," blame, excuse, "the powers that be," "the man," the government, the establishment, the system, and all of those supposed puppet-string-pullers.

Those one in ten thousand who do what they said they would do, even if is building a grossly inappropriate office or apartment building in the middle of downtown, get people believing in them by doing what they said they would do. Whether we like them or not, we are drawn to them because what comes out of their mouths actually materializes. They create as many losses as wins, but we still follow them or give them power over us because they play the game, grab the steering wheel, swing out, and take risks!

Try this—don't say "if only" or "maybe" or use any other conditional language, even if it means talking a whole lot less. BUT when you do speak, make it be to say what you WILL do, no matter what. If you say so it will be so. PLEASE INSERT LOUD WARNING BELL HERE: Bullshit alert! WARNING: many people are walking around saying "what you see is what you get" or "if I say so it is so" or other phrases that may sound exactly like what I'm writing about, but you have to see what they ACTUALLY have produced in the way of results, tangible, touchable, results. These people have been talking crap for so long that they actually believe so strongly in their own B-S that they have begun to mistake words, plans, maybes, and "could-haves" for actual results. Well, this is true to an extent—they are actual results, but the complete opposite of what we're looking for (see long-winded introduction about "honest" and "honesty" being described in some cases by what it is *not*). Wait, the warning isn't over: YOU may be one of those people and not even know it.

Take a breath, get a brown paper bag if you need, and get in touch with the real, real world. A thing either is or it isn't. You either did or you didn't. An explanation is not a substitute. Try this: drive over the bridge that someone planned, started raising money for, took to the planning commission, and only got stopped at the last minute by that damned bureaucracy, through no fault of his or her own. You will wind up in the water as much as the bridge no one ever talked about.

To be honest, as this world goes, is to be one man picked out of ten thousand; that's why he gets the big money—for good or bad.

Simple Exercises for "Honest":

Take the phrases out of your language that dilute truth:

> "Well, honestly, I ...," "To tell you the truth ...," "Seriously, I ..."
>
> For a week notice all of those and similar phrases around you, in your speech and in others'. Break the habit of using those useless phrases (what, when you don't say "honestly" it means you're lying?) and get in better relationship to your language.

When you're with others, notice all the ways that you say what you don't mean, such as "How are you?" "Fine, how are you?" You might as well say "It looks like string cheese today," because no one is paying attention. You can't just throw out all of the social conventions but you can begin to pay attention to how much *waste* comes out of your mouth and work towards a whole new level of honesty and sincerity. Take your time; it's worth it.

Re-do any of the other goal setting exercises in this book like:

> "When the blood burns ..."
> "Brevity is the soul of wit"
> "More matter with less art"

What do you read, my lord?
Words, words, words.

Hamlet, Act II, Scene 2

Don't believe everything you read.

And don't imagine that anything is "true." Why not? There is nothing else in the history of the world that has caused more trouble than people believing that their view is the "true" view; that they know what's *right*. The real "truth" is that peace lies within "being ok with not being right even when you're right" (read that over again—I'll wait).

Here's a true story from my management days: my boss overheard an argument in my office between a manager and an employee. She stepped in, took the situation on, criticized one of her managers in front of the employee, and cleared the room. Not content with her actions at all, I stepped into her office to let her know she had done the wrong thing. She then told me how I had let the situation go wrong, letting the employee go unheard, sticking to protocol over what was practical. I kept harping on the mistake she had made, stepping in and stepping on the situation, disempowering the manager and, in effect, me ("me" is always involved in any situation, isn't it?) After a few minutes of getting nowhere, my boss finally said, "You're right, I spoke out of turn and I was wrong, but that's not the point." I think she had to admit that I was right one more time before I finally got the point she was trying to make. While I was hanging on to being right, she was trying to teach me a lesson in assessing the situation from the "front line" employee's eyes, from the practical side if not the "correct" protocol side, and to question the rules if they don't work, even if she was the one who made the rules.

I was so busy trying to be right, the lesson that was available to me, the lesson about REALLY listening and not living into my preconception, that I wasted a lot of her breath before I began to HEAR her lesson.

Question everything. Break the habit that school got you into: believing all that you read just because it's in a textbook or a newspaper.

Remember that until Galileo published otherwise—and he was excommunicated, arrested, and imprisoned for saying so—the earth was erroneously considered the center of the universe. That was just words, words, words.

Words, Words, Words Exercise:

Oh, my friends, you've been working so hard on this book and its exercises, and it's all just words, words, words. Could you use a break? Ok, here's an exercise that should be fun. Watch a movie. Rent Akira Kurosawa's *Rashomon* (1950).

Watch it with someone else and talk about it afterwards.

I don't have to say any more about it—the movie will be enough.

Journal about the movie afterward so that the lessons go "deeper."

Though this be madness, yet there is method in't.

Hamlet, Act II, Scene 2

"Many a true word was said in a joke."

After the above-cited Hamlet quote comes a quote from my "sainted mother" as we Irish like to say about our late mothers—true or not. There are examples in Shakespeare's plays *Lear* and *As You Like It* of "fools": full-time attendants to a king meant to make him laugh when he needs it. These fools are able to criticize the king's stupid moves and disagree with him when valued counselors are afraid to speak or when the counselors are punished if they do speak up. Political satirists like Mort Sahl, Bill Maher, and Jon Stewart get away with statements that would be slanderous in some cases were it not that they don't call themselves journalists but "comedians." It's a good racket, and we need to laugh at ourselves lest we forget that we're all just making the best guess we can all day, every day, and no one can really tell what's coming next.

There is also a line in a wonderful acting book called *Audition*, written by Michael Shurtleff: "Human beings cannot bear all that heavy weight, they alleviate the burden by humor." At five minutes to 5 p.m. on Friday when your boss dumps a big assignment on you that has to be completed by 9 a.m. Monday, the chuckle that goes with "Sorry to dump this on you, but you know how it goes" is no more sincere than the chortle of, "You don't really expect me to get this done by Monday morning do you?"

At the very least, if you're going to use a laugh or a chuckle to diffuse a situation, use it as a masterful tactic, skillfully applied to allow someone else to "save face" or to give him or her a chance to make the right choice, but don't let the fear of speaking straight, of disagreeing, interfere with your open and honest communication. For some people it is nearly too late—they don't even hear the way they speak through a laugh; they've lost perspective of how much of their personal power, their own authority, that they've lost because they've forgotten how to speak straight.

In short, it's ok if you use it; it's not ok if it is using you.

Madness and Method Exercise:

This is an "awareness" exercise for you to journal about as you observe yourself and others exhibiting this behavior. No "doing" involved, just listening.

For the next few weeks listen and observe yourself and others and notice when you laugh or make a joke as a means to avoid a difficult conversation or conflict.

In your journal list all the times you used this particular device and write out how you could have been more direct, more honest. Feel free to write the actual "script" as it could have gone.

For *bonus points*, go back to the person involved in the conversation in which you "laughed" away your true feelings and apologize to him or her for not being "straight." Let the person know what your true reaction was and commit to being more honest with him or her in the future.

This is an ongoing exercise, so keep it up! Good luck.

There is nothing either good or bad but thinking makes it so.

Hamlet, Act II, Scene 2

Everything depends on your interpretation.

I like crossword puzzles. I like them because they remind me to think in a non-linear way. When I put on my beret and someone says, "Nice hat," I can think of the *NY Times* crossword puzzle and the seven-letter word with the clue "Nice hat." Of course, they are not saying "nice" hat, which could be a "brougham" (but that's eight letters), or "bowler" (but that's five). However, if I think of the city in France named "Nice" (pronounced NIECE), then I realize they are asking me for the French word for "hat": *chapeau*—seven letters.

Now, some people don't like my hat so when they say "nice hat" they're not speaking geographically; they're making fun of me. I can take their ribbing to heart, be embarrassed, and maybe shoot back a nasty retort, or I can make my choice, turn to them, and say, "Thank you, I like it too. It's the most practical hat I've ever owned. I bought it in Paris."

This phrase, "but thinking makes it so," gives you more power over your life and your circumstances than almost any other phrase. This phrase has rumbled around in my brain for twenty years, and I use it again and again. This is the filter I apply to EVERYTHING. In business you can see a breakdown, a problem, a screw-up, a huge loss as a challenge, an opportunity for a breakthrough, or a wake up call that you've been on "automatic" or just ignoring the warning signs. You can make the choice to take the worst event and turn it into a lesson, and it will, could, and might very well be the best thing that ever happened to you!

I heard a Persian story about a man who loved his beautiful pony almost as much as his young son. One day the pony ran off, and the man was devastated. A few days later when the pony returned with a beautiful wild horse as a companion, the man was overjoyed. The next day when the man's son fell off the wild horse and broke his leg, the man was ready to kill the horse—that is, until the emperor's men came through to conscript every able-bodied young man in the village for the army. Because his son had a broken leg, the soldiers left him behind. The man learned to stop judging whether he liked or disliked every single event that occurred in a microcosm but to accept all things as lessons from the universe, some more easily understood than others but all put there to move him along in his journey of enlightenment.

We can all choose to see things as they happen, as factual occurrences in the world, and not attach the meanings that give us childlike joy when we get what we want like a hoped-for birthday gift. When we master our choices, we master our existence, and when we master our existence—well, then fate comes and kicks our feet out from under us to remind us to be humble and to make sure we get over ourselves and take care of the world and others!

Thinking Exercise:

Make a list of everything in your life that you might label "bad." This includes past events too, like deaths in the family, old relationships, mean bosses, failures, etc.

Now, next to every one of these items right what you learned or could have learned from these experiences—the "good" that came from it. You may find it hard to do for some of them: what could the death of a father when you are eleven years old possibly produce that's "good"? Well, self-reliance, awareness, emotional maturity, etc. *That example is my own and I could, and may, write a book on the gifts that the loss of my father gave me. It doesn't mean it wasn't painful and sad; it just is a decision to be _in_ life instead of committed to a "story about" life.*

I could be bounded in a nutshell and count myself a king of infinite space, were it not that I have bad dreams.

Hamlet, Act II, Scene 2

Choose what you have.

What is haunting you? What are you avoiding? Want to be free? Mine the "avoidance" of whatever you are withholding, and you'll get freer than you've ever been. The exercise below is the explanation of the quote. Good luck.

Bad Dreams Exercise:

Make a list. Include all of the things you are angry at others about or want to say but don't have the courage. These are called *resentments*.

Now make a list of things you wanted to do but didn't; want to have, but don't; wished for but didn't take action on. These are called *regrets*.

Now let's take on whatever *judgments* you have about others. This is the one about your aunt who always says stupid things, your uncle who stands too close when he talks, or the relative that your eyes glaze over whenever he or she starts talking.

Now next to each of those items list a 1, 2, 3 or 4.

> 1s are for those things that you will share with the other person, clear the air respectfully, and start fresh.
> 2s are for those things you'll share, just not now, and you'll put a date by when you'll share them (and stick to it).
> 3s are for those things that you are just going to *be right about* and never share with anyone. These are the things you will hold on to no matter what: can't shake it loose, I'm right about it and will be right until I die!

4s are those things that just writing them down, getting them on paper, and seeing them displayed is enough to release them, to let go of them forever.

Now before you go and unload on the whole world, let's create a rule of order. If you are going to share these, ask the person you are addressing if he or she is willing to listen. Let the person know that you are releasing your own opinions, dark thoughts, judgment, and withheld communications, and, even though they are directed towards him or her, *these are all about you*. Let the person know that all he or she needs to do is listen as best as he or she is capable and that your true intent is to remove the barriers between a true connection and relationship with him or her.

Use the phrase "when you do or say X, I think/feel Y" and insert simple, factual, responsible statements.

This is NOT easy, and you should start practicing with people really close to you first so that you don't dump on anyone carelessly. Try one out and then ask for feedback. Do NOT use this as a tool to just dump your own "poop" on others and walk around being right about everything. You can do that without any help from me!

You'll be surprised how much lighter your heart will feel, how your dreams will have less menace and threat, and how your outlook towards others will improve.

The very substance of the ambitious is merely the shadow of a dream.

Hamlet, Act II, Scene 2

Envy is empty. Want is need.

Happiness comes from being connected, loving, and being loved. That is what success is really made of. The shadow of a dream is so empty it is an echo of nothing. Get in life, get it on you, get dirty with it, and don't hold onto some idea of what you want.

I was in my late thirties before I realized that the model of my life was based on what I *didn't want to be*. I was trying to be different, going where no one in my family had gone before, focusing on a life that *wasn't* what they had, and all because I thought "I won't be like them." I guess it's pretty common for the youngest in a family to suffer from that same "non-ambition." It was probably worse in my case because I was the second youngest out of fourteen, and there were so many lives already being lived there wasn't much left over for me—or so I thought.

What I was losing though was what I DID want for myself from a pure, purpose-driven, joyful, and natural organic life "flow." That was when I met my wife. Only I didn't want to know her because I knew that she represented giving up any "distance" or non-involved "watching" life from the outside. I knew what was important to her, saw how she lived her life, and knew that I would never be able to hide my true self from her, let alone ever again be able to hide it from myself. In the process I gave up the "ambition" of being a "star," of giving my whole life to the pursuit of this actor's life that I had seen fail more times than succeed (like the friend I have who gave a child up for adoption and is now enjoying modern success as a comic actress on TV shows—ironically now able to support and enjoy the child she gave up). I wound up getting a real job, moving to the suburbs, blah, blah, blah, tell a really good parable about having three gorgeous, smart children and meeting wonderful, talented people in a whole new area. It's true, but it is still all blah, blah, blah, and I may have just lost you, and I'm sorry.

The truth is that then I started comparing my house to the other people in the suburbs, my mini-van to theirs, my six figures to theirs. Then I had not only my current reality to deal with but the other friends from my previous life who had started to enjoy not only success but fame too! I was screwed in my ambitions, shadow, and dreams and suffered from jealousy, resentment, and anger and still do; that's all there is to it. Don't fool yourself: it never goes away if you have it. And if you don't have it, then it's dormant or you're kidding yourself. (Did anyone notice this book taking a rather pointed turn in an unexpected direction? HMMMM, maybe it's time to get a sandwich or take a break and cool down and come back and pick it up again. Maybe if you re-read the chapter after a breather you'll see it wasn't what you originally thought it was and …)

No, friends, I can't lie to you, because you'll be human—we're human; we're going to suffer the "slings and arrows," so let's be real. But since this book is about a "secret," the "Hamlet SECRET," what have you to offer? I know we're human, but that's no excuse. What can you do? Focus out.

Focus out.

Focus out.

Focus out.

I want you to repeat the phrase so often that it becomes a mantra stuck in your head and so that it comes to you out of the blue when you are your most "stuck." Whenever you find yourself stuck, envious, angry, ungrateful, or plotting revenge, just turn your gaze out and go look for someone who needs your help just this moment. It could be someone who is visibly shaken, close to tears, kicking the copy machine, or holding out a paper coffee cup for change. I guarantee you that such people are out there; you will find someone.

In fact, the worse you have the dreaded "ambition-it is;" the more you may need to focus out. I created an entire volunteer committee with a project a month. Then I added a website geared towards helping people find volunteer opportunities while showing companies the return on investment in supporting and encouraging volunteer activities. I did all of this before I even started to get my head out of my butt (a "recto-cranial extraction" as a good and wise friend calls it). And yet I still am afflicted. But no matter what, if you create service to someone else, if you use what you have to serve those who don't, no matter how far off the track you fall, you have helped someone else. And then that person can help someone else, and then that someone else can help someone else and then ...

Focus out.

Substance of the ambitious Exercise:

Find a soup kitchen.
Work there.
Bring friends.
Be careful that you are not judging.
Smile.
Do the exercise again.
Make it a habit.

Thank you.

A dream itself is but a shadow.

Hamlet, Act II, Scene 2

How about "waking" to life?

Hey, I don't know much, but I do know this—dream encyclopedias use the same model as historical encyclopedias, and we get lulled into thinking they are valid because it is in the book. Words, words, words!

How can your dream and my dream have the same meaning when our lives are completely different, our associations, experiences, likes and dislikes, vary so distinctly? When I see a frog I think "pest" while you may see "pet." Only one letter separates us, but it still matters!

Many cultures see dreams differently. They see our dreams as opportunities for our souls to leave our bodies and wander, meet other souls and loosen the "chains we forge in life" a bit. In feng shui, eastern design theory, you should never have a mirror by a bed because your soul might be scared in seeing its image and abort its nightly mission, leaving you restless and rest-less. Others see dreams as a chance to glimpse the future or connect with our past. They can all be true, and they can all be false, and it doesn't matter. It is all interpretation.

"What dreams may come" is up to us and what we do in our waking lives. It matters what actions we take towards our dreams. If in our beds at night our fears take hold and that new job, new lover, new house becomes a multi-headed hydra with bloody teeth, it isn't license to stay in bed and do nothing! "But I still have bad dreams, so what do I do"? See the exercise.

What Dreams May Come Exercise:

Stop leaving your dreams up for grabs. Immediately before going to bed say a prayer. In the prayer forgive anyone for any harm or ill will he or she may have committed against you that day. Release anyone from any harm or punishment for any sins created against you with an open and generous heart.

Then say, "Thank you, G-d" for all the gifts you have and all of the "things" you've accumulated and do it with a pure and grateful heart. Don't question the events of the day or try to understand them; just review them and let go of them.

Then pray to G-d, not for things, for success, or for anything in particular, but for DIRECTION. Ask G-d (remember you can insert "the Universe" here if it works better for you—don't get hung up on words) for direction in the clarity of the path you should take, in discovering your true path on earth, for the contribution you are here to offer to the rest of the world.

Practice this for a while and you'll see a huge difference not only in how you sleep, but in how you *wake*.

Dormez bien.

If you love me, hold not off.
Hamlet, Act II, Scene 2

Be truthful.

Be kind.

Be truthful.

My truth is not your truth even though my opinion can create such a clever disguise that it looks very much to me like truth when it walks in the door. Then when I am armed with a "truth," I use it to wield the power of the universe, fixing all of those broken people around me and creating the world just as it should be—MY way!

Ok, so it sounds ridiculous, but am I far off from the way it actually occurs? Don't you have opinions that, if this friend or "so and so" would only listen would solve all of his or her problems? And, on the other side of this, is there any good answer to "do these pants make me look fat?" Well, yes, there is a good answer: "No, the pants don't make you look fat. Your big old butt stuffed inside those pants makes you look fat." Ow! That can't be true either. So what can be done? We can't lie to people to make them feel better when they are fooling themselves or harming themselves, or when I want to tell them that I don't like what they're doing or saying. I also don't want to hurt their feelings or damage the family or …

Here is the rule: if you love me, hold not off. Don't hold back; I can take it. If you are taking it easy on me because you don't think I can take it, then you are condescending to me, not challenging me, underestimating me, and I will suffer from it. I might fail if you challenge me, but I will certainly fail if you don't. But do it with respect and care. And if you have a doubt, do it with respect and care and then add a little *more* respect.

Let's put it into a practical scenario. You have a relative with a drinking problem. Is it a problem you have with his or her drinking, or is it his or her problem with drinking? **Respect** allows you to see that others consider a couple of drinks a couple of nights a week ok, even if you were raised on one glass of wine on New Year's and never finished it. **Care** means that you see this person changing into an argumentative person, with a change in "being" when he or she drinks even a little bit, and you know that the person would, if he or she hasn't already, consider driving a car after "just a couple." Respect and care then says you have to challenge him or her about it.

Respect and care says that maybe you should ask for advice and guidance anonymously before acting (that is considering the situation isn't imminent and life threatening). Respect and care means that you write down and rehearse what you will say and try it in front of a mirror, constantly checking to see if you believe yourself, if you are really, really being present in the moment.

Respect and care mean you do all you can to deliver the communication at the right time, in this case when the person hasn't had anything to drink, or in the right place; don't ambush the person at home or invite him or her to yours under false pretense. Say "we need to talk." Respect and care mean you accept that what you think, your opinion, is yours and is naturally filtered through your own life and that you ask permission before you speak. I think you get the rest of it, don't you?

Just use respect and care and do your best. Practice responsible communication, but don't shy away from difficult topics. Be a good friend and risk losing a friendship if it means not losing a friend for good.

And don't use "self-righteousness" as a club to wield against others—but if you have respect and care, you know that already, don't you? Good luck with this one—you know what I mean, don't you? G-d bless you.

Hold Not Off Exercise:

There is no real "exercise" for this one: it's a really loaded topic and one to be considered with caution. Think about what I wrote above and the one person or circumstance, yours or someone else's, that came to mind as you read this. Spend some quiet meditation on that. Consider what is best to be done or not to be done. Most importantly, "Reck your own reed" (see "Do not, as some ungracious pastors do …") and take care of yourself and your health of mind and body.

This chapter I leave up to you and G-d to do what's best.

What a piece of work is a man.
Hamlet, Act II, Scene 2

People are complex gifts to the world.

Think about it: each second every part of this machine we call a body is working at its jobs. Your heart is pumping, veins and capillaries are regulating blood flow, central nervous system is checking all systems and making little corrections here and there, skin is regenerating, food is being turned into waste or energy, and complex thoughts and actions are working in harmony to produce a PBJ sandwich or a new symphony. And do you have to "think" about breathing, your heart pumping, or digesting to have it happen, or does it just happen whether you think about it or not? Cool, eh?

You may have seen this before, but let's ask: what happens if you lose a leg, G-d forbid. Are you still you? Now the worst happens and you lose both legs. Then both arms are lost. Are you still you, at the core? We could shave off bits and pieces of body parts and still come up with the same you INSIDE. You can have a machine put in for your heart, and people who are brain dead can live on for years, and who knows what is going on with them. What IS you?

Well, maybe you could stop trying to add or subtract anything for a while and just BE you. You are not your head, your arm, your shoe, or foot. You are a perfect being trying to tread water when you could float. Stop the struggle and just BE the you inside, the YOU that IS, whole and perfect no matter what the outside form, the clothes, job, car, spouse or partner, or any of the trappings we add on. Just allow the YOU inside. That YOU is clear, perfect, and only needs your peace, acceptance, and "flow."

Piece of Work Exercise:

Find a quiet space and sit still. Let your brain run where it will, thoughts go where they will—don't try to channel them, empty them out, or make this into a Zen lesson. Just sit still. Set a clock for ten minutes ahead of time if time's an issue. You may fall asleep—could be you are tired, so sleep a bit. But just sit still for the five to ten to fifteen or so minutes, as much as you can manage. Then get up; get on with what you need to.

The next day, and as often as you can, sit still. Let the machine do the work. It really doesn't need you that much, does it?

And yet you struggle so much and work so hard. Hmmmmm.

What a piece of WORK indeed.

I am but mad north-north-west.
When the wind is southerly, I know a hawk
from a handsaw.

Hamlet, Act II, Scene 2

We all have our days. Watch that.

Listen, it is easier for me to repeat again and again what others have written or to make this an obvious and predictable *Hamlet Soupçon for the Soul*, but let's get real again; we're all emotional creatures, and as much as we can handle, we have to knock it off. Barring the complete acquiescence to our "watery side," we have to create awareness around it and handle our emotions responsibly.

There are so many, many books and practices out there that guide us around concepts such as "we are not our emotions," "we are not our feelings," etc. that you could create an encyclopedia of them. Erich Fromm first wrote about how in the English language we say "I AM sad," or "I AM happy" while in other languages, like French, we say "I HAVE sadness" or "I HAVE happiness"; the French and other similarly linguistically constructed languages distance themselves with their words from being consumed by what they are feeling at the time. We all can have our feelings without falling victim to them.

Now I admit that feelings are a real phenomenon; they are valid, they are necessary, and they are hugely preferable to their opposite, but let's get real about them. Let's say you are feeling sad and you decide to stay home from a meeting you had set up. Then you begin to feel guilty about canceling the meeting. Next you feel worse about yourself because this reminds you of all your similar past transgressions—further proof that you are inherently bad and weak, and the sadness gets deeper. Instead of an "up to the ankles" sadness you are soon treading water above your head. Whatever mechanism you have to cope with these feelings then comes into play, and out come the cigarettes, booze, drugs, chocolate, ice cream, racing forms, credit cards, fast food, porn, or compulsive TV watching to dull out your feelings, to anesthetize them, and you begin to numb out.

That works, doesn't it? What's wrong with that? If you went to the doctor's office and said you had a pain, he or she would give you something to take to numb the pain, right? Of course, but the doctor would also want to diagnose the cause of the pain. The symptom, the dis-ease, becomes the disease becomes the cancer, if left untreated. But diagnosis creates awareness, and *awareness* is the blessing <u>and</u> the curse; once you have it, you can't get rid of it.

Awareness is realizing that you have an emotion, that you have pain, and that you can make a conscious choice of how to deal with it. If you consistently let your emotional "madness" direct your actions, you'd soon be in a straightjacket. Own your emotions by claiming them. If you are ready to blow up, try "claiming and exclaiming," "I am so mad I could kill you" and then get out of there until you can tell a hawk from a handsaw.

Go for a walk or sit down in a park and do a check in—close your eyes and notice where the anger is in your body. Is it tightness in your stomach? Is it pain in your forehead? Instead of numbing it, dive into it. Talk to it or talk about it. When was the last time you remember feeling this particular sensation? What was going on? When was the first time you remember feeling this particular sensation? What was happening then? Find out what "button" is being pushed, take responsibility that you are allowing yourself to go down that tunnel, and then ask yourself, "Is there any light down that tunnel?"

"Well, we're HUMAN, and humans are going to feel, and feelings are real, and they need to be honored and ..." Ok, I get it, and you're right. But that's what discipline is about. Do you think the Jewish laws of Kosher are as easy to explain away as that in our early society eating pork or shellfish, etc. was a health risk? If that were so, then all the non-kosher-observant societies would be extinct and Jews would be the plurality of the world instead of a small minority. The observance of discipline in small matters, of watching everyday urges and appetites, are the moral equivalent of working out, exercising, and practicing in advance of a big "game" or "match." Try a little discipline in one everyday, non-conscious part of your life, like chewing a bit slower when you eat, taking a deep breath every time you look at your watch, etc. You will soon develop, with practice, a discipline. You'll begin to get present, and a whole new view of the world will open up. You'll have more days of "southerly" winds.

Now as to being MAD north by northwest, it is good to go a little out of control now and then. It is good to have passion, to feel deeply our emotions and to follow where our nature takes us. Just don't claim to have no power over them or use them as an excuse to be a jerk.

And G-d forbid you read this, find you can't even begin to sort out those emotions and know now that you lose yourself over and again to your passions. If that's the case then get help. Get a coach, a spiritual advisor, a doctor, or a therapist until you are in a better state to handle it on your own. I mean, just the fact that Hamlet could say he was mad sometimes was proof that he was sane enough to have awareness!

Hawk and Handsaw Exercise:

Step 1:

We started above with a few small practices to make us more conscious.

Take a breath every time you look at your watch. Inhale, exhale, and notice how you're feeling in that moment, how you're holding your body, sitting, etc. Spend a moment or two just doing a personal inventory and on each exhale allow a little release, a little tension to escape.

When eating, try chewing each bite of food one hundred times before swallowing. Taste the food and even close your eyes as you chew just to notice all the machinations of chewing, salivating, tasting, and digesting.

Schedule a walk in the outdoors at least three times a week and use the time for walking meditation.

Journal about what it feels like to "diffuse" with these small practices and what awareness it engenders in your daily life.

Step 2:

Take a look at your schedule for the coming week. Are there any appointments that you really have strong "feelings" about? Are you afraid of any of them? Why? Do you "hate" any of your appointments for the week? Are there things on your "to do" list and calendar that you "love" to do?

Without changing or canceling any of the appointments, try to change your feeling about them. If it's fear, get to the root of the fear and take it on. Are you unprepared? Get prepared. Do your homework. Is it a presentation and you don't like speaking in front of others? Get coaching or search the Internet for the tips and tricks of public speaking. At the very least, spend some time visualizing the best possible outcome of your presentation, how you'll look and feel if it went phenomenally, and let yourself project a "win."

If you hate any appointment, then take that on too. I'm not sure we can cover all of the causes for that one here, but one way to deal with this is to ask yourself if there is any benefit you get out of this "hated" event. No one I know likes a root canal, but it's better than chronic pain, infection, and gum or bone disease! If, however, you find yourself hating most of your appointments or your job, then it's time to share with someone else, get coaching, or tune up your resume.

Now I might go easy on you and suggest that you look ahead at the following week and, with the benefit of time, cancel anything you hate or fear, replacing those things with things you love, but that's a complex matter and not part of today's "lesson." Is it a good idea? In general, yes. But before you can go there, you need to do most of the exercises in this book and not let yourself off the hook—we have to face our fears sometimes, and some of the things we hate to do we have to do in order to grow. Really that's too complex to take on now. Start with creating awareness and being conscious. Otherwise you'll drive yourself crazy!

Use every man after his desert and who shall
escape whipping?
Use them after your own honor and dignity.
The less they deserve, the more merit is in
your bounty.

Hamlet, Act II, Scene 2

Is that the "golden rule": Do unto others …? No, it's a bit more than that. It means you should actively call on the best in people. You should see them as their truest, highest, selves and pull that towards you. If you consistently do that you'll soon be surrounded by people showing up as their best.

A good friend and coach uses "declarations" with the people he works with. You create a statement, "I declare that I am …" and then finish with "You can count on me …" The declaration is a statement of being, and if done right it should be calling out the *you* that you *will become* by doing the work, getting conscious more each day, and taking the better choice more often than not. There is no good or bad, right or wrong in it, just a statement. For instance, you might declare to the rest of the team that you are "passionate, inspirational coach, creating a clearing for breakthroughs and extraordinary accomplishment." If you say, "You can count on me to create a safe environment for growth, sharing, care and respect," then you are committing to everyone around you that you will work towards that too.

Now if you already ARE these things, are already creating breakthrough results in an environment of care and respect with the people you're working with, then you have to "up the stakes." But if you ever fall from that path, the others around you will have a place to stand in order to call you back to your goal. And you will do the same for them. Having created the statement, you are creating the permission for them and you to be that thing and to call on that in each other. When you are interacting with others and they are being their "Diabolical Declaration"—another fun part of the process where we declare how

83

we can (and will) show up as our worst just because we are human—we have another chance for awareness.

We win by looking for the best, no matter how intent others are to show us their worst. G-d knows there are enough occasions, enough instances, and enough people who would allow us to indulge our darkness, and some actually feed off of that to gain their own "dark" power and keep others around them small. Me, personally, I'd rather be surrounded by giants and know they're on my side.

Know each person has a light inside. Look past the darkness, find the light, share your own (and it may need to burn brighter if the other person is really lost in his or her own darkness). But the rewards ...

"Merit in your bounty" Exercise:

Think of someone important in your life that you are having a hard time with. I don't mean the worst example or someone who could be arrested for what he or she has done, just someone who brings out the worst in you when he or she is around, either always or just recently. I'm talking about the one who just gets under your skin by being in the room. Got one? I know you do ...

Now for a week, spend journal time each night writing about the good in that person. Ignore the bad about him or her and only focus on the good. Keep writing the same thing over and over if that's the best you can do, but keep it up for a week. Expect a miracle.

Murder, though it have no tongue, will speak with most miraculous organ.

Hamlet, Act II, Scene 2

Ease up, judge, jury, and executioner, and try pardoning every now and then.

Consider this example: you are mad at someone who has done something wrong, and it's just not right that he or she did it. You think the person needs punishment because he or she may do it again or do it to someone else or … I mean, *it's the principal of the thing*, isn't it?

Maybe you're right. Maybe you are a judge and it is your job to decide what punishments people should get. Are you a judge? Maybe it's your workplace and the person keeps lying, or you can't count on him or her and a lot of other people feel the same way. Well, if you're the manager then you have to take care of your team. Are you the manager?

For most people, except the actual judges and managers, it gets pretty frustrating having to see people be "bad" or get away with murder. They need punishing or to be just "fired" or go away. Don't they? Listen, owning your experience of the matter may be the best you can do, and whether you know it or not, you're not perfect either. At best we'll let go of our judgments and the awful weight of trying to control others, trying to mold them into our version of "right" or perfect. Letting go of that weight alone will free you in ways you can only dream of now. They'll pay their own price, and you don't even have to be involved. It's happening right now.

One more thing: try loving the people you now judge. I won't explain how to love them. Just try. Understand, accept, and love. Go ahead. I'll wait.

Murder's Miraculous Tongue Exercise:

Practice taking your communication to another level. The next time you doubt someone else's honesty, don't just come out and say, "LIAR!" That would just put him or her on the defensive and create more drama: "You don't trust me," "You never believe me," etc. Instead, try saying something more truthful but less confrontational: "I'm not comfortable with your answer. Can you help me figure out why I might feel unsure?"* Do it in the moment, as it happens or as you learn about it. Limit your comments to the incident at hand. If you are feeling that you just don't trust someone, then try letting go of judgment and taking the onus off of him or her. Tell the person, "I feel that you withhold things from me; that you don't share all that you're thinking, and I'm sorry about that. In this moment right now is there something I'm doing that makes you uncomfortable?" Try to stay in the present moment and don't go back into the past, as it's too late. Find a way to speak your truth in the moment and remember that the person is reacting to who YOU are being, and in the "Land of 100 Percent Responsibility" (see chapter "**Let my disclaiming from a purposed evil ...**'), you gain power in your life by examining how you are the cause of others being dishonest with you. How are you treating this person that he or she doesn't feel able to confide in you?

Be ok with nothing new happening in the chosen conversation or with the chosen participant this time. This exercise calls for a bit of mastery you may not yet possess (and it is difficult even with mastery). What might also be happening is that you've planted the seeds for the next conversation, the one where honesty and a new level of open sharing are possible. Expecting the best in people and letting it come to be on the other's timetable is one great way of loving others.

*The exact wording is difficult because even my example sounds a bit condescending. Don't try for perfection; use your own words, add YOU to the script, and do your best. That will be enough for me because after all, *I'm* not judging *you*, am I?

The devil hath power to assume
a pleasing shape.

Hamlet, Act II, Scene 2

Handsome is as handsome does.

The "devil" is the dark force that keeps you from pursuing the perfect, clean and remarkable human being you are. It is the force that accuses you of being not good enough, not smart enough, not whatever enough. That is the real devil.

The devil wants you to think you stink and then shows you specific instances where you actually do stink: sins, misdeeds, laziness. It has these pleasing shapes like chocolate, coffee, cigarettes, alcohol, staying up late, favorite TV shows, or indulgences like the Sunday morning *NY Times*. Now most of these things won't kill you in moderation, and they seem worth their pleasure, but you have to have a bit of discipline and self-control to make sure you are the one in charge and not them!

What we're working towards here is to see what we do when we are "up against it"—what crutches we rely on. Once we stop our habitual patterns in order to see them clearly and their effect on our lives, we take back our awareness. This way we can shake off a little numbness from ourselves. We'll see, too, what we never realized was a defense mechanism or a stress-reliever, those "trigger" events where our impulse bypasses our conscious brain (just barely). EVEN healthy things like working out or going for a walk when you're stressed can be overdone, and it is very necessary to be able to find out what is the root cause of the stress—what have you not dealt with, and why not?

The devil is in there telling you not to wake up, not to create awareness, not to realize that when you're doing something self-indulgent, something to relax or blow off steam, that it's ok, natural, and sometimes a good idea. But without awareness, present-mind thinking, you could still be living on top of pain or fear that the devil wants you to keep on avoiding. This pain or fear can't be named or exposed because it might be remedied, and *if you begin to erode the habitual, unconscious and un-dealt with or hidden fear, doubt and pain then ...*

By the way, these "sedatives" can be used to keep you from doing what you said you would do, and this can be deadly too—like the medication that says "don't take this pill in combination with alcohol," etc. If you said you would sort your closet tonight but you really don't want to because you worked hard today or you had a bad day or some other reason, the devil will say, "Ok, relax. You're right—you don't need to keep your word *all* the time, do you? You can't be *"perfect"*! You DESERVE a little break every now and then, don't you?"

Listen, it is true that things come up, you need a break now and then, and we are only human and can't be robots, but you have to know we sell ourselves short. And we do it with things that look pretty good at the time, and then years down the line we look back and say, "When did I grow so fat/soft/lazy/habitual, etc?"

Some of those "shapes" the devil assumes are so pleasant that we don't even recognize that we're allowing them in or choosing them. Do the exercise below and create awareness and then ask yourself: does this serve me in living a passionate life? Does it serve me living true to my purpose in life? Is this what I really want? Am I "in life" or just coasting along, numbed and happy on the surface, longing and craving on the inside? It doesn't need to be so dramatic either; everyone can afford a little more awareness and a little more self-knowledge.

Devil spelled backwards is "L-i-v-e-d." If you are "coasting," you are living backwards; you haven't lived.

Devil Exercise:

Stop doing things that you like. I know that sounds crazy (and it is) but "try this on." Leave quitting cigarettes out of this exercise if you're a smoker. Actually you should just stop smoking, no kidding, but we are going to give you a "pass" on butts for this exercise. We'll take some things not so hard to "kick" for most of us. Pick your "pleasing shape": alcohol, chocolate/sweets, TV

Alcohol: Try spending three months without a drink of any kind. Can you do that? There's no "need" to drink, and many people live their entire lives without it. What's three months in the bigger scheme anyway? Just "cut it out."

Cut out chocolate/sweets for a couple of weeks or a month or just on weekdays or something that doesn't *kill* you but that is a REAL stretch compared to your current consumption.

Give up one night of TV a week for three months. You can DVR any shows you want; just don't watch them for three months. If you do that you're just adding more TV time at a different time. Just go "cold turkey" on any shows that air for one particular night per week.

If none of these are your "thing," then choose whatever that "thing" is that you crave when work gets tough or the world just seems to be out of control. Check your memory for moments when you felt like you *needed* a drink or an emergency chocolate fix or realized that you'd just "zombied out" in front of the TV for three hours straight.

You can combine "pleasing shapes" over this period too. Pick two things that you use as "numbing agents" and put them on hold for a while. Eventually you can make this "laboratory" of pleasing shapes a normal part of your life. It will keep you present and awake; these are good things.

You'll notice I'm not suggesting any replacement substance or activity for any of these things. The danger in "replacements" is that they could be just another "pleasing shape" and we'd learn nothing. For this exercise it doesn't matter what occurs when we get the "urge" to indulge in a pleasing shape. What matters is "cataloguing" the urges and noticing what impulses occur that want to go right past your conscious mind, leaving the pain or fear un-felt or unregistered. It is important that you journal around these impulses as they occur or as soon after as possible. Get to know what makes you tick, and whirr, and hum, baby. Your life is worth examining.

Important NOTE: If you do suffer any symptom of withdrawal, any unusually uncomfortable or uncontrollable response to this exercise, then it is up to you to seek professional help. I don't mean getting grumpy because you haven't had a chocolate in three days; I'm talking about being responsible for your health. You'll know what I mean—and don't let the "devil" give you a "back door" either. Get help if you need it.

Whether 'tis nobler in the mind to suffer the slings and arrows of outrageous fortune or to take arms against a sea of troubles and by opposing end them

Hamlet, Act III, Scene 1

Worry achieves nothing. Action produces results.

A sea of troubles is usually all of the things we have been avoiding. It is the stuff we didn't want to deal with now, the sure and certain future if we didn't change our track, the consequence of fearing rather than facing.

Take Arms Exercise:

Do a "gut check" and pick the one thing in your life that isn't working, the one *outrageous fortune* that is keeping you under its thumb. Use the "five whys" technique from systems management. Write the issue on a page in your journal as a statement like "my car is about to croak." Then ask at least five honest "why" statements consecutively until you get at the root problem. You may have to do it several times to get the hang of it, and you might get benefit from asking a friend to help.

From "my car is about to croak" comes:

1 Why? The engine is running hot, and it's making a clunking noise that gets louder every week.
2 Why? I haven't had time to take it into a mechanic, and I'm afraid it will cost too much to fix it.
3 Why? I don't want to spend money on the car that I can spend on something more useful, and I don't have enough money as it is.
4 Why? I keep thinking my life will change; I'll get a raise, bonus or promotion; and then everything will take care of itself.

5 Why? Because I just haven't wanted to accept what's so in my life, here and now, and have been living in a dream. I haven't been doing proper maintenance on my life, either, and I keep thinking that clunking noise in my head will go away too. And because **I hate this car** as it represents the mediocre life I'm living.

In five really honest "whys" you can begin to get to the in-authenticity of any situation, the root cause of suffering in the mind: the thinking, worrying, trying to figure out, put up with, endure, etc. Cut out the suffering, get out of your head, and go for a swim in that *sea of troubles*. They never really end entirely; the waves just seem to lose their power a bit as you "take arms."

The native hue of resolution is sicklied
over with the pale cast of thought, and
enterprises of great pitch and moment with
this regard their currents turn awry and lose
the name of action.

Hamlet, Act III, Scene 1

Greatness comes from action.

You can convince yourself not to do anything if you think about it long enough.

I met a woman named Val who was not afraid to mention that she was safely in her sixties. In her early fifties she had been faced with no husband, and the business she worked for was being sold; she was out on her butt. As she needed the money, knew the business pretty well, and had built up some good relationships, she decided to put everything she had into a garden implement business. By the time I met her she had about five people working with her and was looking to spend less time working and turn more of the day-to-day operations over to a manager she had hired. Things were going very well, and she could consider herself a success.

Now the part I like about her story is that when she needed to form a business she didn't have any time to waste, so she just went out and did it. Then, after the business was in swing and she could take a bit of a breather, she went to a Women in Business support organization so she could take courses on starting up your own business; accounting, legal, etc. What she told me was that if she had taken the classes before she started her business, *she never would have started her own business.* If she had gone to school first, she would have been convinced that she couldn't do what she had *just gone out and done.*

I keep Val's picture around to show to anyone who ever comes in and is *"thinking"* about doing something instead of going for it.

The Name of Action Exercise:

Go online or go to the library and get a book about someone who achieved great things. Read it. Let his or her example into your soul. It doesn't have to be Winston Churchill, Mahatma Gandhi, or Mother Teresa, by the way, to inspire you. There are countless examples of "normal" people who've built a small shop into an empire, followed a passion or a dream. Find someone who "took action" and let him or her tell you about it. Be inspired to be in action. Get out of your head and into your life.

To the noble mind rich gifts wax poor when givers prove unkind.

Hamlet, Act III, Scene 1

What is the most important gift you can give anyone? No, but "diamonds" are a good guess; let's try again. The answer I am thinking of is "you"; giving of you, your time, your heart. Now don't be too literal on this and think that you have to be a boy/girl friend, spouse, lover, etc. to give of yourself; that's small thinking. What you give might be a few minutes of really great and intense listening. You may make time in your schedule to attend an event that is important to someone and thereby show support. You might buy his or her kid's Girl Scout cookies even though you are on a diet or allergic to thin mints. What is important is that you "said" in actions and in a gift of time: "you matter to me."

Now how can this be "unkind"? You can screw up any great action or gift by expecting thanks of any kind or gently, no matter how tactfully, reminding someone that it is an expense you pay on his or her behalf. That is like making a donation to a cause just for the tax write-off; technically it works, but it is not actually good for your "soul."

A quick note on giving as I used the example above: the Great Rabbi Maimonides, one of the wisest men of all times, said that the highest level of giving to another is not just giving freely. It is not giving without expecting anything in return or anonymously. The greatest way to give to one in need is to give in such a way that you support the person never having to rely on others again. It is empowerment that gives the most to the world and to others.

Giving of yourself to others, a rich gift, that creates a sharing, a connection, and a sense of being a part of a greater whole, creates another human being who understands what it is to be wholly alive. It is not your ego you serve then; it is the whole world.

Rich Gifts Wax Poor Exercise: three parts

1. Take out your calendar, PDA, or other scheduling device.

Add a recurring appointment, at least once a week, to call someone in your family, a friend, a former colleague, or someone in whom you are or were personally invested. This will be a different person every time, so call the appointment "Rich Gift." When this appointment comes around, call people from your life as suggested and tell them you were just thinking of them and wanted to see how they were doing and what they were up to. Seriously be prepared to listen without distraction for twenty minutes to a half hour. If you can do this in person, then it is all for the better. Get in the habit of doing this once a week or every other week, whatever you can fit into your schedule, but do it. If the person asks about you say, "I called *you*, we can talk about me the next time when/if you call me. Right now it's all about *you*."

2. Find someone in your office or home who is working on a project, up against a deadline, or who seems to be struggling a bit. Get him or her a cup of coffee or a candy bar or offer to bring something back for lunch. Give freely of what you can and let the person know you notice how hard he or she working. Tell the person you just wanted to acknowledge his or her effort. Say it simply and without drama and then leave the person to his or her task.

3. Create a random act of kindness or beauty. I used to type up little notes to co-workers to point out moments when I saw them exhibiting new leadership skills, patience with a co-worker, or some small extraordinary behavior. I'd slip the note into their mailbox without signing it and encourage them to do the same for someone else. Do something great for someone else and do it anonymously. Put this in your calendar too, as often as you can, but put it down on paper so that it can move from a "good intention" to a reality in the world.

I am myself indifferent honest, but yet
I could accuse me of such things that it were
better my mother had not borne me.

Hamlet, Act III, Scene 1

Nobody's perfect. Or are they?

I have had this one come up several times in the past few days and was a little surprised how common it is. People think things and feel guilty for them, as if there was something wrong with them. They think they are their thoughts!

Let's try it: be your thought for a moment. Try thinking yourself a huge white bird and fly around the world in a second. It's not working; think harder. HARDER! Still not working? Hmmmm. If you thought it and it didn't actually happen, then if you think that you'd like to strangle that little brat next door who just got the drum set and who thinks that 7 a.m. on Sunday is a good time to practice, loudly, badly, and for at least an hour … Uh, oh, go check the kid out and make sure that … No. Nothing happened to the kid just because you thought about kicking holes in the drum skins as you covered your head with your pillow.

As we've said in earlier chapters, you are not your thoughts. You are your actions, your consistent actions. You think it's a good idea to give to other less fortunate than you, but unless you give donations regularly and in keeping with your fortunes then you are lying to yourself and living in a fantasy.

You are not your good thoughts or your bad thoughts but because you *think* others will *think* something about you because you're *thinking* what you're *thinking* you will keep inside of you what you're *thinking*. If you don't admit what is going on in your head, clear it out, say it out, admit what you WANT to do without doing it you will only keep adding fuel to the fire. You'll never be able to let that thought out of the little gerbil wheel of a brain you're creating. Got that?

And by the way, most of the time, someone else is thinking something very similar to you. Once you see that, you can give yourself a friggin' break for a change.

Get off the guilt trip; it's a long ride with no final destination.

And if your mother had never borne you, then you wouldn't be able to accomplish for the good of the whole world what you came here to do! So get to it!

One last thing: no matter what you've done, every sinner has a future and every saint has a past. Deal with both with courage and create today the yesterday you'll look back on with pride tomorrow.

Indifferent Honest Exercise:

Let's try this. Create a little prayer. When you find yourself about to "blow," about to yell, or about to choose the "wrong path" (i.e., something you normally would feel guilty about later), try saying the prayer. It can be a secular prayer if you want that doesn't invoke any particular religious allegiance, or it could just be counting to ten.

Then, each night as you journal, go through the events of the day and review those things you wish you hadn't done or wish you hadn't said or that make you wince just thinking about. Write them down in a list and then, next to each item, write "I forgive myself for this," even if you can't feel the forgiveness now. At the end of a week or so, review the lists you've made (one each day) and notice how they're beginning to lose their hold on you. After a week of this you should be able to "get it" that we're all human and that the true goal is to choose the "right path" more times than not.

Tough break that "being human" part, but there's nothing to be done about it. You'll just have to keep doing the work of growing in the face of all that that means. But after a while, it does come a little easier. A little.

Madness in great ones must not unwatched go.

Set an example.

Let's take a trip to Nadia. Nadia is a massage therapist with an amazing sense for what it takes to be healthy. When you get on her table you are in for it—in a good way.

I met Nadia when I was suffering from a stiff neck that had passed the "pain in the neck" stage and was affecting how I viewed things and people around me. I was grumpy and realized that I had to get some relief from my pain.

When Nadia asked how I got a stiff neck, I was honest with her: I was choosing to be *stiff necked* about what was going on at work. We had some changes going on in my office, and I had been avoiding some really difficult conversations. As we dug in to our office breakdown I found myself being "right" and judgmental, opinionated and stubborn. The metaphor for being stubborn and prideful is "stiff necked." Metaphors DO mean something, and they all come from wisdom older than memory; it is a good idea to listen to them.

Nadia guessed that the pain in my left shoulder was really the result of a shift in the way I was holding my right side, and she was right. I had had a minor surgery on my right foot and, as Nadia put it "I was out of balance." Now I was out of balance not just in the fact that my left shoulder was about a half inch higher than my right, but in the way I was "holding" my life and my "now." I was angry with so many people, so much of my situation, and I was being such a righteous jerk about it that something had to give sooner or later. Think how funny it was that I couldn't turn my head to one side; I could only see one side of me—of anything.

Unfortunately it took more than this realization to "cure me" and Nadia's care was only the beginning of my healing. I had totally "screwed my *self* up" and "getting straight" with things and people was a step-by-step recovery. But at least I was on the path to being back in balance, getting "even" with myself.

Madness Unwatched Exercise:

Put yourself on Nadia's table. She begins by looking at your body to see where the obvious tension is and where you're "holding," but you have to get naked first. She'll tell you if you're being too tense, too tight, too strained and whether or not you're out of balance.

Start the exercise by writing out a few simple metaphors for how you are feeling physically. (If none come to mind immediately you might want to start the list with "numb.") Once you've listed out a few of the sensations, try to "self-diagnose" with the old metaphors freely to see if you can figure out what is going on in your life, how you are "being" that is leading to your physical manifestation. Spend some time journaling on all of this.

Part 2:

Now let's get out of your head and into your body.

> Schedule a full body massage. Schedule them over time if you can afford it.
>
> Pick up some Epsom salts and sea salt and follow the directions on the box for a relaxing, detoxification bath.
>
> Go to bed an hour early for a week or at least change your pre-sleep ritual to include reading a book just for enjoyment (I know you enjoy reading work-related topics, but I'm asking you to let loose a bit).
>
> Add any other elements here that you'd like that achieve the goal of caring for your physical self: relaxing tensions, soothing aching or sore muscles, and in general getting in touch with your physical self. Indulge.
>
> Go ahead. I'll wait.

Let your own discretion be your tutor. Suit the action to the word, the word to the action.

Hamlet, Act III, Scene 2

Live as your word.

To be known as a "man or woman of your word" is no easy task: important, yes, easy, no. Do it anyway. We've dealt with integrity in "brevity is the soul of wit" but let's do a quick refresher. Integrity is not "right/wrong," "good /bad," etc., but rather "is/isn't," did/didn't. If you say something will happen by a certain date, then commit to having that happen. Don't commit to anything smaller than you can accomplish. Play as big as you know how and keep stretching what you "thought" was possible. Being in integrity is having what you say will happen actually happen.

So what happens if you say something will happen and it doesn't happen? The answer is "nothing"—in many senses of the word. The thing you committed to won't happen and, as so many people are used to a world where people don't live their word, most people don't expect you to keep your word anyway so they may not even call you on it. So let's try something else on.

Let your discretion be your tutor: from now on commit to really listening to what comes out of your mouth. Really listen to every "thing" you say, all you put out in the world. When someone asks "How are you?" don't just say "fine" or "great" without really considering it. Most people who ask "How are you?" are not interested in the answer anyway, not listening, as if they were just throwing their words over the edge of a cliff and wasting the chance to connect with another human being. If you answer them truthfully or consider your response, you may just slow them down enough to have them actually get present in their life for one short moment. You may just connect and really spend a sincere moment with another person. Note well: I don't mean that you should come up with some pithy response like, "If I were any better I'd be two of me" or anything in the egotistically obnoxious category like that—far from it.

Let Your Discretion Exercise:

This is an ongoing practice. If you say you will do anything, no matter how small or seemingly inconsequential, (1) *write it down and put it into an existence system like a calendar or a computer software program like iCal or Outlook*. Make it a real commitment and have it happen. For example, you say to someone "let's meet for lunch soon." As you hear your potentially empty words—"soon" can mean "never" if misused—stop and create a real agreement. "Forget 'soon,' let's make a specific lunch date right now so that we make sure we actually do it." And if this is someone you really don't want to have lunch with, then don't say, "Let's meet for lunch soon"—it's a lie, isn't it? If he or she says, "Let's meet for lunch soon," then challenge with, "If you really mean 'soon' then I expect you to call me by next week with an actual date and time, ok?" Then it becomes that person's opportunity to let your discretion be *his or her* tutor and, unless you have a tone of voice or a "come from" of being right or better than him or her, you have a chance to make the person feel connected or that he or she really matters to you in that you actually want to make "soon" happen.

The added plus to this is any of the people that actually do follow through on their word to your invitation are the type of people you want to have more of in your life. At lunch, make sure you acknowledge them for keeping their word! Actions that gain praise are apt to be repeated.

Let your discretion be your tutor (2); go back and consider anything that you have said to anyone in your past like "one day we'll go fishing" or "I'll make a date with you" or even something as mundane as something borrowed and not returned. Then *suit your action to your word, your word to your action* and (3) call the person involved and clear it up/clean it up. If you borrowed something and it has become like yours—worn, broken, or lost—offer to replace or return it and make some form of restitution or "interest" for the inconvenience he or she has had to endure because of you.

Get people seeing you as a person of your word, and people will start listening to what you say. The "down side" is that once you begin living your word people will expect it of you—you will be called forth, so to speak, as a person of integrity. You will be as trusted for what you say as what you do, because the two will be inseparable. The good news is that this "down side" is just you being the you that we are all meant to be, and while it makes life a little more difficult at times, it also makes it a heck of a lot more worthwhile. Each and every moment begins to take on a very tangible "weight."

One last note: if you are living big enough in commitments, then you can't help but fail sometimes. Something you said becomes impossible or needs to change for any reason. When this happens, you need to acknowledge it, clean it up, and recommit. Don't beat yourself up or lose heart.

What's most important is that you have a clear, clean, and honest relationship with what you say will happen. Let your discretion be your tutor; if you find that a lot of what you say with the best intention is still not happening, then you need a reality check—a REAL reality check. Get someone else to "hold the mirror up to nature" and pay attention to what he or she says.

Give me that man that is not passion's slave, and I will wear him in my heart's core
Hamlet, Act III, Scene 2

Don't imagine the worst but don't over-dramatize the best either.

"Passion's Slave" is someone who dreams *the big dream* while regretting "what's so." These are people who think they've missed the boat somehow in creating the life of their dreams and spend their time on "what if" and "what's the worst that could happen?" How would it be to feel in touch with your "heart's core" desire and not be passion's slave, a dreamer waiting for some dramatic turn of events for life to really have "meaning"? Two concepts in one, in some ways, but they're very strongly connected.

If you could put your life into perspective, you would be free. You would be able to create a big possibility to live into, and you would create it now, in the very life you are living. You would know what could happen, and you would be able to respond to threats and urgencies appropriately. You could be free.

You would be free.

Passion's Slave Exercise:

Imagine an elephant ...

No kidding, that's the way one of our exercises starts. In a seminar we create a fantastical creature, half purple with orange circles, the other half orange with purple circles. Where we go from there is up to each person's imagination. Did I say *imagination*? Remember that? Maybe you, like most adults, don't know where you currently keep your imagination. I'll tell you where it is: you've put it on assignment to create worry and various "the-worst-that-could-possibly-happen" scenarios. In our seminar we create the elephant to re-awaken the proper use of the imagination: creating the biggest and brightest future. We rev it up a bit with the elephant to get it ready for the next part of the exercise.

Imagine that the next year of your life was yours to do anything you desired. Money and time were supplied as needed, and your regular responsibilities to work, spouse, children, parents, etc. were suspended. What would you do? Ok, you may want to indulge yourself a bit in the "never shave, lay in the sun, sleep all day and watch sports/go shopping" stuff for a while, but let me know when you're done with that. Done? Yes, that *can* be fun, but it is not really what you would do; it's what you *wouldn't* do. It's your first reaction, and it's like bingeing after spending years starving so there's nothing "wrong" with it; it's just not your heart's desire. It's your brain's desire in a knee-jerk sort of way.

Now let's go to what you would do if you could change the world. How would you change it? What would you create that would carry your name and legacy forever? What would you do if you knew you only had one year to live? Are you beginning to see the elephant?

Now, since there's no real offer on the table that means you have a year of freedom in the sense I've described it in this exercise, no one should be quitting his or her job right now or running off to an ashram with family and financial responsibilities left hanging. It's an exercise, remember? Where to go with this next is to see how you can have the *idea* of your heart's desire right now in your present circumstances while letting go of the need for everything to be perfect first. If, for example, your heart's desire is *ending world hunger,* then the way you can have a piece of that now is by working weekends at a soup kitchen, putting food donation bins up at your workplace, or contributing money from your job no matter what you do for a living. You can indulge your passion and be responsible at the same time.

Start using your imagination on ways that you could be in service to the world, how you could have, in your present circumstances, everything possible in your heart's core.

I want you to be in action, and I believe in following your dreams. But we're all connected, aren't we? We all play a part in each other's dreams, and we don't need to be passion's **slave**. Slavery: bad. Service: good.

The violence of either grief or joy their own enactures with themselves destroy.

Hamlet, Act III, Scene II

Keep the drama to a minimum; keep the play within its theme.

The symbol of Yin and Yang suggests a perfect balance of two opposing forces as a worthy goal to achieve. So does the creation of man and woman in the Garden of Eden. To achieve "health" of any kind we need opposites like man and woman, dark and light, Coke and Pepsi. However, too much of anything causes an imbalance that doesn't serve anyone. The overindulgence in our victories or our defaults causes us to lose the lessons, build up blind spots and, in general, lose the edge that living with awareness offers. Try the exercise for a better understanding.

Violence of Either Exercise:

Create a chart on a page in your journal with two columns. Label one column "good" and the other "bad."

For the next two weeks put all of the "happenings" of your life on the list under one of the headings.

After the two weeks is up go back to the list and reverse the column headings.

Look for ways that the good news can actually wind up "bad" and vice versa, for example: "found $200 in an old sport coat." Bad: shows carelessness with money. Money could have been used for charity or for a gift or as investment. Etc.

Then after two weeks just list the events on one column.

After each item write the "good" that came from them and the "bad" as well, plus what you've learned or will do with this information in the future. In our example above, for instance:

"Found $200 in an old sport coat."

> Bad: shows carelessness with money and the money could have been used for good, invested or donated.
>
> Good: I used 50 percent of the money to donate anonymously at my place of worship and used the rest to treat my wife to an impromptu night out "just because."
>
> What I learned is the "fun" of finding money. I'm putting a few $20 bills in an envelope in my home file drawer and purposefully forgetting about it. I'm including a note to my future self that when I find this money again I should use it to take a friend out to dinner to say "thank you" for something he or she has done for me or just for being a friend when I needed one. I will leave it alone long enough to actually forget it; in fact I've done this one before and left it in a place I'm sure to find it within the year so there's no danger of it being lost forever. See what you can come up with for yourself.

Make it fun.

'Tis a question left us yet to prove, whether love lead fortune, or else fortune love.

Hamlet, Act III, Scene 2

Open yourself to the flow of the universe, even if somehow you need to pry the door open with a crowbar.

There is a responsibility to a relationship. There are days when you are totally in love with your partner and days when you would leave him or her in an instant. It is human nature to be up and down—though if you or your partner are too often up and down then see a doctor—but you need to realize that you are not your feelings or your thoughts (how many times have you read that so far in this book? Well it's true, that's why!). You are your commitments and your actions that express that commitment.

Some days it is easy to just "go with the flow" and it is easy to be in love.

Some days you have to "fake it till you make it."

Keep your commitment clear and present; it is your way to fulfill your soul's purpose. You were put here for a reason, and if you do not fulfill your mission then no one else can and it will be left undone forever. It has to involve someone else, doesn't it? Start with the one person in the world who chose you for his or her very own.

Love Lead Fortune Exercise:

Ok, this one is *so* easy, and you may already be doing it. Allow me to make the following suggestions anyway.

Buy a box of pretty cards and envelopes. Give yourself some time alone and write a few little notes to your spouse or partner. Make the statements timeless but not schmaltzy. Tell him or her what is your favorite part of his or her body and why. Describe when you first realized you were "serious" about him or her. Write his or her name on the envelope and hide them in places your partner only visits occasionally so that he or she can find them over a long period of time.

Add a "coupon" for extra value. The coupon offers anything from a night off of usual "duties" like washing the dishes, to a back rub or foot massage. You can add anything you'd like to the coupon; it's up to you (just be cautious in case anyone else might find the card). Sexual coupons are ok; just don't limit yourself. Intimacy has many facets, and they all count.

Set a "date night" and put it into your calendar. Once a week? Is that enough? You know that a lot of nights you just feel like coming home, kicking off your shoes, and doing nothing, but the danger there is that it can be habit forming. Make it an appointment and keep it.

The most important issue of all is that you create the "fortune" of your relationship with purpose and intent. You may be just naturally "lucky," of course, but why take the chance, eh?

Our thoughts are ours, their ends none of our own.

Hamlet, Act III, Scene 2

You can't call back what you say, so think about it before it flies too far!

Sometimes the distance from your head to someone else's can be the longest distance of all. That's because the way starts out slippery before a trip over jagged "rocks," followed by a flight in the air and a target that is a very small hole leading to a narrow canal. Once your words make it past all of those obstacles, they run into a machine that is only 10 percent working at best. So how do we stand a chance communicating our true thoughts and being heard in any form close to our original intent? Slim chance.

How to get the odds more in your favor? As in any game, rules make it easier. Here are a few rules to get you started.

- What role will you play? When someone comes to you with a problem, start by asking what he or she wants from you. "Do you want advice or do you just want me to listen?" Play by the rules and honor his or her requests. The world will not stop if you just listen one time instead of offering advice.
- Stay in the now. Treat every conversation with others as if you just met them. Take care with your words that they're straight and to the point. Don't embellish or assume—pronouns, "you know," "kinda," etc. are so imprecise and can lead to warped communication. If it's important enough to say it, then deliver it with care and respect for both of you.
- Stay in the now. Don't carry the past into an argument. "You *always* do this," "You never do that," etc. How can anyone stand a chance to make a change when you bring his or her whole history into every situation?
- Ask if you've been heard. "Did what I just say make sense?" "I'm not sure if I'm speaking clearly. What did you just hear?"
- Take a communication class; don't just rely on these few words. They are a starting point, not enough at all to really give you

mastery of communication. I mean, think of it—slippery path, jagged rocks, small hole, and a narrow canal into a machine that only works about 10 percent!

Our Thoughts Exercise:

Tape up on your desk or your home office the five "starter rules" I've given you in a place where you can refer to them often.

Go online and find a communication course; sign up for it.

Go over the "Our Thoughts Are Ours ..." exercise and redo it if you haven't done it in a while.

If you work in an office, put a sign over the entry door to your office that says "What do they need from me?" and do your best to be a generous listener, a masterful communicator.

Get in the habit of taking a pause before you answer any question; try counting to ten and then speaking. It seems a long time when you're inside looking out, but to most people listening, they'll hardly notice the pause.

Keep it up; it's a lifelong effort, and the rewards are worth it.

The lady doth protest too much, methinks.
Hamlet, Act III, Scene 2

How much time you spend denying is directly proportional to how much you really don't mean it.

The story is like this: if one person calls you an ass, he or she is probably taking something out on you, so let it pass. If two people call you an ass, then you're probably just in a bad mood or in the wrong place at the wrong time. If three people call you an ass, buy a saddle.

Feedback, good or bad, is data you can and should use to judge how effective you are in your milieu. You mustn't take it too personally or you'd be a useless, quivering ball of jelly constantly worrying if people like you. Trying to be liked is a major cause of unhappiness and is simply your ticket to inauthentic-city.

On the other hand, ignoring what people say and feel about can lead to loneliness and could be the result of an over-inflated ego. If you find yourself in that situation, feeling like people are avoiding you, feeling like people don't like you, then test the feeling by finding a life coach or talking to someone who will give you direct and straight feedback.

If you find yourself saying, "I don't care what people say," too many times, then you are probably in difficult straits; it's time to get real.

Protest Too Much Exercise:

Take a poll.

Create a list of ten questions similar to this model. Before you begin, tell the people you are interviewing that this is a self-assessment tool, a personal inquiry, and invite them to be honest. Pick three to five people who know you well. Don't pick people who will gladly take you apart, but don't pick people who will sugarcoat it either. Mix the contexts of your life as best as you can: work, friends, family. Again, setting the context of allowing them to be heard so that they're comfortable sharing honesty is a big job, so take it seriously. Take your time and be grateful; you're asking people to be honest in a way that isn't "normal."

Would you name one or two of my strengths?

Would you name one or two of my weaknesses?

On a scale of one to ten, ten being the highest, how would you rate my "honesty" level?

If you could change anything about me, what would it be?

Would you describe me in at least one but less than three sentences?

If you had advice for me, what would it be?

Do you find me a good listener?

If I created a new business and invited you on board, would you work for me? Why or why not?

How am I talked about when I'm not in the room? You may need to give some assurances on this one—people may not want to "gossip"—be ready to negotiate on this one.

If you were the casting director for a movie of my life, who would you cast to play me? (This is surprisingly revealing at times but also a chance to end on a little "fun," so don't get too serious on this one—have fun!)

You may have a dud interview in the bunch, and you can do as many of these as necessary. The key here is to interview your "subject" as if you were talking about someone other than yourself: listen and don't defend, rationalize, or self-congratulate. Be an impartial auditor and give a generous listening. Change the questions if you like, but it's best to do them in person and allow time so you're not rushed or "getting it over with."

This is a rare opportunity; savor it.

You do surely bar the door upon your own liberty if you deny your griefs to your friend.

Hamlet, Act III, Scene II

Ask for help when you need it.

Why do we think that asking for or needing help is a sign of weakness? Could you imagine thinking it demeans you not to be able to stitch up your own three-inch gash from that rusty tin can or taking out your own appendix? Yet when we have a problem or a persistent sadness and someone says, "Are you al right? You seem sad," we almost automatically respond, "Oh, it's nothing." How often do we think we can figure something out on our own, from taxes or financial planning, to our careers or vacations?

Certain people have certain passions, ideas, and proclivities, and they are given these gifts to serve others. In exchange for serving others, they gain a reward of satisfaction, pay, or some other value. NOT asking them to help is denying them the full expression of themselves, and that means you've shorted out the full cycle of energy you were meant to be a part of. And that is just for taxes, financial planning, vacations, and careers!

Friends and family, on the other hand, are not just making an observation; they are trying to help, trying to connect and be "with you" as you are. If you can't be generous in accepting their offered hand, then you are really denying the light of G-d, the Universe, the flow of all that you deserve in life, and it is just plain old, selfish behavior! Ow, eh? And you thought you were being selfless and heroic in bearing your burden all by yourself! NOPE. Reprogram!

And that's not all ...

117

Bar the Door Exercise:

For the next week you're going to say "Yes" as often as you can. Who are the "angels" sent to you every day? Find out. For instance, the other day I was looking at various snow-melting materials in the local hardware store—a place I'm pretty comfortable in. As I stood there, another shopper walked past me, put his hand on a bag of ice-melt, and told me, "I bought this one, and it works pretty well." Then he just walked off. I'm sure he was an angel sent to me in that moment—not that I was in distress, just sent to me for the ordinary and everyday.

For the next two weeks, watch and listen for people who are sent to help you in ways large and small. Say "yes" when someone says, "Try this out" or "That looks good on you." Journal about what you notice, the price you pay for saying "yes," the new experiences, even the small ones, you'll have when taking guidance from the universe.

By the way, sometimes YOU are the angel. Did you ever have an "impulse" to take a different route, take a shortcut, or go the long way around? As often as you can over the next two weeks, listen to your "inner angel" and then see what comes of it. Be open to see what you might not have seen; hear what you might not have heard, before.

By the way, you're saying "yes" to me—I'm one of those angels if you'll let me be.

Call me what instrument you will, though you can fret me, you cannot play upon me.

Hamlet, Act III, Scene 2

Don't react hastily. Respond "responsibly."

Do you know what it feels like when someone is "pushing your buttons"? Do you realize that you are allowing that to happen? Of course you do! You *don't?*

The first step is, of course, awareness that your mythical "button" is getting pushed. Once you have that going for you it all gets easier. The way to handle that is to do a "check-in" every time you feel yourself getting upset or "triggered."

Fret Me Exercise:

Try this: the next time someone says something that rubs you the wrong way, something that is like nails on a chalkboard to you, especially if it is a recurring issue, then substitute another word for it. If it is your mother who always uses the word "lazy" to describe you, think that she is saying "rhinoceros" or "butterfly."

Then: Do a quick body inventory and see where you are feeling the strongest reaction to the situation. Are you holding your breath just a little bit and tightening your chest muscles or stomach? Are you clenching your teeth or clamping your jaw? Is it in your finger- or toe-tapping? Once you've identified your tension—it's funny that we talk about mental tension in stressful times but don't extend that into checking our bodies for where it lies—once it's clear where the tension is manifesting, just do the opposite or embrace it.

If you want to try *doing the opposite*, if you notice tension in your chest or stomach, then take a deep breath or five before you respond. If you want to *embrace* tightness or tension, then exaggerate it purposely by increasing your tension or holding your breath as you tighten every muscle in your body.

Post note: Using the exercises above and those that you'll discover out of this awareness might help "short circuit" your usual action-reaction cycle and give you back your ability to choose your state of mind or emotion in each circumstance—OR you may just choose to be in what you're in and take what's coming; there has to be some payoff to that, right?

My words fly up, my thoughts remain below.
Words without thoughts never to heaven go.

Hamlet, Act III, Scene 3

Be sincere.

How often do people say they are *sorry* and then repeat the offense? Often.

Saying "I wish that didn't happen" or "I wish this wasn't true" doesn't make it so either does it?

Sincerity comes from your actions matching your words.

Consider what it is that actually creates the behaviors in the first place and then take that on.

Let's talk about lateness as an example. If you are chronically late, the pattern is usually that you arrive late, you apologize for being late, you intend never to be late again, and then the next time … What is going on is that you are comfortable with *the behavior that leads* to lateness. That is what it all comes down to, isn't it? Comfort. There is more *comfort in the behaviors* that lead up to the result of lateness than the discomfort with the *consequences of lateness*.

For you to actually break the pattern and create a new behavior you have to get *uncomfortable* for a while. Getting uncomfortable for a while will eventually pay off. Breaking a pattern or habitual behavior increases awareness and gives a greater sense of authority over your own life: the dis-ease can cure the disease.

Words without thoughts: (This one you may just HATE.)

Set your morning alarm for one hour earlier than usual for one week (weekdays should be enough). Do what you want with the time; just don't waste it. Journal about both the discomfort of getting up earlier and any benefit you get from it. After a week it's up to you what comes next, but at the least you've gained five hours in your life. See if you can overcome the *dis*-comfort and gain something positive.

One week. One hour per day waking earlier.

Upon the heat and flame of thy distemper sprinkle cool patience.

Hamlet, Act III, Scene 4

Control your temper, or it will control you.

Ok, we've addressed this here and there before so let's just go for the simple tools. Count to ten!

Remember when you were in kindergarten and the teacher told you not to hit and even suggested you count to ten before reacting? Well, it worked then, and it will work now; just be a little more subtle.

Exercises/Practices for DisTemper:

Calls—before you pick up the phone and give someone a "piece of your mind," call a trusted friend and ask if you can (1) *"vent."* Define "vent" as just blowing off steam at him or her without any need of him or her offering advice or opinions. Your friend's part can be just to listen and stop you if it goes on too long or gets too violent.

Can't get a good and trusted friend on the phone? (2) *Vent on paper.* Write the letter you would send to say exactly what pisses you off and get it all out there in every bloody, gory detail. Then rip the letter up no matter what. Even if you agree with what you said as you read it on the paper, make yourself write it again or better yet, wait until tomorrow to re-write it.

Ready to talk to the person upsetting you? (3) *Write yourself an outline of what you'll say.* Making pre-conversation notes is always a good idea when it's something important, but in terms of anger or disappointment it is a necessity.

If it's an email, do all the same as above and avoid at all costs hitting the "send" button until you've waited a few hours or considered that "there are more things in heaven and in earth" then you have considered.

Suppose a space alien really IS inhabiting his or her brain: then how would you approach the person with a new understanding for his or her "meshugas"?

And by all means lock up the booze in all cases of upset: a stamp licked with liquor lips will never produce a sober result!

Confess yourself to heaven. Repent what's past. Avoid what is to come; and do not spread the compost on the weeds to make them ranker.

Hamlet, Act III, Scene 4

Break the pattern and the habit of what's stopping you from integrity.

EVERY single day you get to wipe out what came before and re-create yourself. No matter how much sin you've committed, no matter how much pain you've caused, today you can choose to be different. Every saint has a past, every sinner a future.

But you don't just get to wake up tomorrow and say, "To heck with what I've done to you or anyone else, I'm free and innocent." That would deny responsibility for action. Find those you have wronged, where appropriate, and ask forgiveness. If you "owe" them anything, then make it up to them as best you can. If they say "no way," then you've asked your pardon and the holding on is theirs from then on. Do not decide that you have ever gone so deep into that hole that you still can't shake it off, grab the first rung of the ladder, and climb from inside the hole to being whole (as in a whole and balanced being).

Before taking this on, it's best to ask for support, like a coach or a dedicated friend to be involved as you attempt this. The Alcoholics Anonymous Twelve-Step System gives good guidance on this, and it can be irresponsible to try and achieve this step on your own. Don't keep repeating the behaviors that you know to be painful and harmful to yourself and others—it could be too late one day.

Confess Yourself Exercise:

Make a list of everything you regret doing or not doing.

Add to the list all of the people involved.

Next to each of the items write down a remedy or means to "make up" for what you've done or not done.

Take all of the items and plan out your calendar of recompense.

NOW take it easy: bringing it up again or reinvesting in an old hurt could cause pain for others. Sometimes it's not enough to say "I'm sorry" nor is it a good idea. You have to know the difference between seeking your own peace of mind and doing good to others with tact and sensitivity. Consider that what you need to do for someone you've hurt is a random act of kindness. Send a random bouquet of flowers, give to charity in his or her name, or send the person a portfolio of lottery cards or "Scratch and Win" cards.

Note: If you stole or chronically owe money, then a lovely greeting card, of course, won't cut it. You'll have to pay back the money (or arrange to pay it off as best as you can in larger cases), but *there's no "I'm sorry" and forget-the-debt pass* here: money is money. There may be hurt, anger, etc. involved as well as money, and those can be handled too—should be handled—and that can be handled separately.

Ask someone you trust to help you plan this out, someone who won't sell you out to make you feel better but also someone who won't make you drag yourself through the mud.

You will notice a new sense of freedom for every act you undo—guaranteed.

Assume a virtue, if you have it not.
Hamlet, Act III, Scene 4

Act "as if," even if you don't "get it" yet.

There is a story of the Jewish people at Mt. Sinai. G-d had approached all other nations and asked them if they would be his "chosen people" and enter into a covenant with Him. You should understand that "chosen" has pretty much the same meaning as "volunteering" in the military. It means duty and responsibility, work and devotion.

As the people had no concept of what it would mean, G-d "helped" them make up their minds by picking the entire Mt. Sinai up and holding it over their heads. Faced with the option of having a mountain come crushing down on them or accepting the deal, they accepted the deal.

The problem was that no one at the time had a concept of what the covenant with the Almighty might mean. Since there was no way for them to get what was happening, they made the following pact: "We will do and we will understand." They agreed to follow the rules *before* they got them.

As it turns out, rather than the worst deal ever made, this was probably the best. How is that? The idea that our brains, our limited minds of which we rarely use more than ten percent, could totally drive our lives, that our minds could fathom the great mysteries unaided, is insanity. As the (in)famous Werner Erhardt of EST fame said, "Understanding is the booby prize." Trying out new modalities, new practices, new behaviors is a sure means to grow. If you want breakthrough results, in short, you need to take on breakthrough steps. You need to do some "faith" work.

Assumed Virtue Exercise:

Take any exercise from this book—preferably one you've previously done and possibly the one you liked the least. Read it over one more time and then "back track" your notes and journaling on the experience. Give it another try. What I mean is: repeat the exercise, and this time do it just for the sake of doing it. Don't think about what it will give you, what you'll gain from it, etc. Don't agree with it or disagree with it; just do it. If this is the first exercise you've opened the book to, then just flip the pages randomly and do the exercise on the page you happen upon. Come on—it actually gets fun!

Use can change the stamp of nature, and either master the devil or throw him out with wondrous potency.

Hamlet, Act III, Scene 4

Correction: Yes, you CAN help it!

Try this: Schedule something you've been putting off. Not just something like doing your taxes, but an 'enjoying your life on a new level' event. I mean, what are you waiting for?

There is an old, old, joke about a guy who goes into a diner and asks for a rotten egg, stale toast, burnt coffee, and a moldy cinnamon bun for breakfast. When the waitress asks him why he wants this "bad" food, he says, "I have a tape worm, and that's good enough for him." Ha, Hah.

We all have some version of what we deserve and what our "due" is. Somewhere along the line we created our *worth*, and we hold ourselves to it. We may not be worth much, so we don't do much or allow ourselves much. We may think we never deserve more than our parents or more than our neighbors. We rise to the level of our "use." Can't we change that?

Where many parents wish more for their children than they ever had themselves, the children don't always accept it. We could be and can be happy, healthy, and prosperous, despite the self-limiting core beliefs we try to hold on to. Let them go. Let yourself go too—to the next level. You are worth it. You are worth it. You deserve whatever you put your mind to, and anything is possible. Anything is possible. You're not hearing me: ANYTHING is possible.

Stamp of Nature Exercise:

Take out your calendar and put one self-indulgent event on it. Start with something small like calling and arranging a massage once a month, for example. Schedule shopping for new clothes *before* you wear out the old ones. Plan a vacation to some place you've always wanted to go. Find a better-paying job. Talk to a financial planner or invest in your future so that you'll have greater wealth. Treat yourself like someone you were trying to impress or woo. Journal about the feelings that come up when you do this, not at the end of it, but as you set the schedule, as you keep the appointment, after you keep the appointment, etc. Change the behavior that results from the limit, and the behavior will shift the limit. It's all in your mind anyway!

Anything IS possible.

Be thou assured, if words be made of breath,
and breath of life, I have no life to
breathe what thou hast said to me.

Act III, Scene 4

Don't gossip.

What we hear firsthand, or experience firsthand, is real, and we can speak of it. Nothing else is in our ability to speak of. Once you say or hear the words "he said" or "she said" or "I was told"—you can fill in the rest of this long list—you are on "thin ice." It takes a great deal of discipline to say, "Stop and let's do a check in here; do either of us really know this for absolute true?" If you can't say you were there or involved personally, then you are giving in to that most human addiction of drama diving. Some twisted gene in all of us says we need extremes of "juicy tales" like small doses of what soap operas churn out so readily.

If someone tries to draw you in to gossip, don't get all righteous and "high horse" about it—just remember to see the best in the person who is trying to gossip and you'll know what to say.

Here's a story I heard: A congregant gets angry with his rabbi and begins to spread lies and stories about the rabbi's virtue. As soon as he cools down and sees how wrong he was, he realizes that he has to clean things up with and endure the shame of confessing his actions to the rabbi. The rabbi listens sincerely and offers to forgive the indiscretion—for a price. The rabbi hands the congregant a well stuffed feather pillow and instructs him to take it to the edge of a cliff on a windy day and to let the feathers blow in the wind till the pillow is completely empty. "When you have collected every single feather back from where the wind has taken them, then we can forget this episode." You get it, I'm sure, but once gossip leaves your mouth it follows a path you can never predict or control.

After a while of resisting gossip, life just seems easier, really.

Words Made of Breath Exercise:

Shut the "hell" up.

Sorry, I am deliberately poking at you with those words, but it's not what you think. The "hell" is the stuff that works in your head in certain circumstances with others. The "hell" is what you say as part of the role you play in your group, your life, your family, even when sometimes you instantly regret what you said. So, just to give you an idea of what has been coming out of you, I want you to just shut up. The next time you're in a group of people, just be quiet and listen. Listen to what people say. Observe without judging. Hear the type of things people say about others. Notice what they add as far as opinions, embellish what they heard, or joke about at others' expenses. Just listen. Sure, someone might mention that you seem quiet, but just say, "I'm just listening," and let it be.

Good luck. Let me know what you notice, would you?

We fat all creatures else to fat us, and we fat ourselves for maggots.
Act IV, Scene 3

You can't take it with you.

Well, this is inglorious but true: we are all going to die. We are all going to decay in the sense of our bodies. In light of this, we can be hedonists and consider all the living creatures of this earth here to be served with drawn butter or basted in garlic and olive oil. After all, the universe and the world were put here to serve *us*, right?

Recently I watched a documentary in which drone cameras floated through the deepest parts of the seas, the middle of nowhere in the deep below the poles. The level of sophistication, variety, and order of life that exists in places we are totally unaware of, are out of contact with, and which we would normally never see—and this is just in the "observable" world—is absolutely mind blowing. If we come from the mindset that man is the center of the world, the reason for the earth, the master of nature, then why are all of these other creatures in place in this huge "zoo" if we never or rarely meet or greet them?

As far as any directions that came with the earth, I remember man being given the task of *naming* the other animals (being the only creature which would CARE that animals had a name) and that he was given "dominion" over them. It is a matter of choice of definition, but "dominion" can either mean "control," or it can mean "protectorate." So, since EXTREMELY few animals actually bend to our wills or ever have bent to our mastery, then the evidence would tend to say we have the latter definition to work from.

Our "job" is not to eat, abuse, or use up the other creatures of the world but to consider why would we want to name each and every one *if we were not to love and care for them.* I mean we NAME our children not to sort them one from the other so much as to make them unique, create them as individuals to love and care for; we're not going to keep them as "pets" until the day comes for us to cook them up.

And one thing else: what kind of karmic sense of humor would make the huge, ego-driven, terrestrial leviathan called MAN wind up in a box in the earth as food for one of the lowliest, simplest forms of life there is? Get it? Come on, get over yourself and get it, Worm-food!

Fat for Maggots Exercise:

Time for your "Hundred Things to Do before you Die" list.

This is a little different from the exercise in "Why as a woodcock ..." and "Springes Exercise" where you add to the list things that you've already done, creating a kind of "curriculum vitae"—remember that one?

This list is one hundred things that you will do from now until the end of your life. Make it big and small, make it real, and make it meaningful and fun. For example, on my list are things like "buy my wife a BIG diamond," "get an award from the mayor," "go skeet shooting," etc. but there is also "end world hunger."

Now pick one item from the list and do what it takes to cross it off as complete. Keep it handy, and whenever you're contemplating a little free time or a new venture, take out the list and check it before committing to anything new. I've had one for about five years now, and I've taken quite a few things off of it; it feels great.

Let's all get busy, ok?

What is a man, if his chief good and market of his time be but to sleep and feed? A beast, no more.

Hamlet, Act IV, Scene 4

Pursue your purpose in life.

It is perfectly ok to just take life as it comes and do what feels good in the moment. It is ok to go to work, come home, eat and watch TV, go to bed, get up, eat breakfast, and start the whole cycle over again day after day, including watching sports and sleeping late on the weekends. It is ok—for a while. But who wants to look back on his or her life on his or her deathbed and say, "I guess I lived a pretty 'ok' life"?

The problem arises when this pattern is repeated so often that it becomes a "rut" and you forget what it was in service of. What was the dream you were pursuing or the vision you sought after? Was it really just to earn enough money to live in a nice enough place and wear nice enough clothes, eating and drinking pretty much what you want? Maybe it's all right for a while, right? But not forever.

Beast No More Exercise:

Try this: draw a series of circles on a paper with a small one surrounded by a bigger one, surrounded by a bigger one, etc. You should wind up with four circles in a target pattern.

Now write down in the smallest circle **how you affect yourself**. "I like me, I work out, I buy a new article of clothing once a month and read ten books a year."

Now go to the next bigger circle and write **how you affect friends and family**. "I go out with my buddies every Friday night." "I call my parents once a month and visit them twice a year." "I helped my cousin write her college entrance essay."

Now the next "ring" is about **how you affect your community**. "I give a dollar to the homeless guy outside the coffee shop once a week." "I go on the summer volunteer day with my office mates on one Saturday in August."

Now the biggest ring is for **how you affect the world**. If your responses are like the examples I made up above, then you might not have that much to write in this sphere, but don't leave it blank.

Now start the exercise again and fill in the circles:

- as if you were your childhood hero
- as if you were you with the energy of when you were a teenager or younger
- as if you were the friend who you are always jealous of
- as if you were the person you've always wanted to be but gave up on being as you started experiencing REAL life (ha to that one!)

Keep doing this exercise until you come up with at least ONE thing that you will do for your community and the world *that excites you to the core*. If you can't find it, ask for help. Just know that it is inside you and you will be a "beast" until you find a way to actually be in action on something you discover here.

I do not know why yet I live to say
"This thing's to do," sith I have cause, and will,
and strength, and means to do't.

Hamlet, Act IV Scene 4

What are you waiting for?

It is with a wonderful sense of irony that I approach this quote; I don't want to take it on as it is *so* big. Well, here goes: we have created this *myth of ourselves*. In our myth we are capable or incapable, a sum of the appraisal of all the events that have come before, a sum of the input from others including parents, teachers, friends, and enemies. These are all part of our myth.

Some people have the myth that they are successful in all things, and that is then true. Others have a myth that they are bad or wrong: this belief can be on the surface, deeply buried, or even masked as "something other" like a series of bad habits. On this list of habits consider things like drinking too much alcohol, eating for comfort, or making unconsidered remarks at inappropriate times. And these are then true.

The truth (there's that word "truth" again!) about the myths is that they are true if you say they are. "Right you are if you say you are" is actually a title of a play by Pirandello, and it really rings true. We all function on proof that it takes this and that, combined with that and this, in order for this and that to occur. In fact, we can point to countless times when *this, this,* and *that* came to be <u>this</u> or **that,** and that's the way it is, isn't it?

Then someone comes along and does exactly what can't be done because along the way *no one took the time to tell the person that what he or she had just done was in fact impossible.* If only the person had known it was impossible, he or she wouldn't have just gone ahead and done it!

There is no time, no circumstance, no REASON involved in what your heart tells you needs to be done. G-d is giving you the clue, and G-d will give you the power to do exactly what it is that your heart knows must be done (if you don't like the word "G-d" in the preceding just insert the word "universe" and get to it—forget semantics).

In short, if it comes into your head to do it, then you are equipped to accomplish it. I do not make this one up, and if you want to get on the phone and ask me to give you examples of times when this has exactly occurred in my life I hope you have free long distance minutes, because it could take a while to tell them all!

This thing's to do Exercise:

Go to the library and take out a book about someone who went from rags to riches. Read it. ***Horatio Alger*** is the classic example of this model, but try finding someone from your hometown or closer; a real person, not another "myth," is best.

After you've finished reading the book, recommend it to someone else.

Then start asking people you know about people they *personally* know who have done the improbable or better yet, the impossible. Call these "I'm Possible" people up, tell them about this book and your exercise as a context for contacting them and ask them to meet for lunch. Over lunch ask them to tell you their story and listen to it. Thank them and then go out and get to your "myth." YOU should pay for the lunch, by the way; you're the one who'll get the "dessert"!

Rightly to be great is not to stir without great argument, but greatly to find quarrel in a straw when honour's at the stake.

Hamlet, Act IV, Scene 4

Choose your battles.

Face it: the little things bug you, but you don't want to make a fuss of it. In order not to make the fuss, you hold back, you "eat your words," or you "smile and be a villain" because you don't want to "get into it" or "make a big deal," etc.

Well, do you remember the story of the peasant who on his deathbed called his three sons to his side? He asked them each to bring a stick along. As he held one of the sticks separately he showed how easily he could break a single stick even in his poor health. Then he bound all three sticks together, and even the strongest son couldn't break them.

The lesson of that story has a different intention than what I am getting to here, but it can be applied. If you get in the habit of being honest about every little thing, to the "eyelash," you can take it on. If, however, you allow the little things to build up too far they may just break you.

Now I'm not encouraging you "going off" on everyone all the time for every little thing, but I am saying to be honest and in the moment. If you think you are being treated unfairly, you can register how that makes you feel "not ok" and say just that: "I'm uncomfortable with this conversation and the direction it's taking." Whatever happens from that point on is going to happen, and we can't go too far into it here, but at least you've been "real" and put your discomfort on the table.

Another tool is to say, "I don't agree, but I am willing to align." Especially in a work environment this can be a useful tool. You have noted that you are not in 100 percent agreement but that you will go along with the team for the sake of the whole. Don't take this too far and align with anything morally unacceptable, of course, but "let your conscience be your guide."

Still another tool is to check in that you were understood and heard. As long as you are sure that you got your point across and it was heard, considered, and measured, then as an adult you can say, "I don't need to be right, I just want to be heard," and then move on with your life. You have to know that things won't always go your way. How boring would that be?

Using these tools and developing more tools like this will allow you to be a highly functioning team member. The payoff is that the more times you can practice these disciplines, the more people will be able to hear you when it is really important.

Quarrel in a Straw Exercise:

Revisit the "Meet it is I set it down ..." chapter and add these practices, extending the practices you've already begun.

Revisit "Though this be madness ..." chapter too.

O, from this time forth, my thoughts be bloody or be nothing worth!

Hamlet, Act IV, Scene 4

Live with urgency, not emergency.

What's the difference? When you know what needs to be done, when you are clear and sure, then no expense is too great. You must do whatever it takes to make it happen, and that means you may dwell in discomfort and take a great risk. But the risk is commensurate with the reward in most cases, so why play smaller than that? How many times do you hear people saying, "I wish," "If only," "If I had it to do over again …" etc.? TOO MANY TIMES!

As I tell my coaching clients, once you have decided something will happen, all the ways it *can't* happen will come forth. All your fears will surface. All the people whose job it is to tell you how you can't do it, how others have failed under similar circumstances, how much you stand to lose, etc., will suddenly get an urge to call you and keep you *in line*. If you are moving to a new situation, the old one will take on a new sheen, a new luster, and things that make it not "so bad" will randomly occur. And they all have in common the same desire: to keep things the same because "same" is safe.

Well, as they say, ships are not made to stay in the harbor. But how can you tell the difference between a good idea, a crazy impulse, or a misguided ego desire?

Bloody Thoughts Exercise:

Write out whatever the question or issue you are facing on the top of a big sheet of paper—for example: "Should I start my own business?"

Then write what you are **thinking** about it in your head. Write your thoughts, your intellectual "take," what you think, what you know, what you consider, and *what a smart person would do,* etc. Use every "thinking" or head-centered metaphor you can draw on to journal about your decision.

Then write what you **feel** about this new venture in your heart and soul. Write your experience "from the heart" and include what you fear. Write about the passion it inspires and include all the "feeling" type statements you can.

Next is your **"gut"** reaction. It can be difficult to prime the pump for this "gut" part because we can tend to ignore this useful part of our decision-making process. (Deepak Chopra writes that the enzymes or peptides of digestion are chemically the same as those produced when we think. The difference is that our stomach has never evolved "self-doubt"). State the issue again and again and write down your first "gut" reaction to it. Make as many statements on this list as you can.

Now go back and consider which of these three realms offers you the most encouragement and freedom. Whichever one it is, that is the one to draw your courage from. It should be the dominant "force" in facing this issue.

This exercise can yield powerful results in a group setting with a facilitator, but just journaling it will help you a lot. Don't skip this step and, once complete, "get moving!'

Refer back to **"There are more things in heaven and earth, Horatio ...'**

We know what we are,
but know not what we may be.
Act IV, Scene 5

Dream big! But BE big now for real power.

Power can be defined by how many times what comes out of your mouth actually occurs in the world. It is having the commitment to say what you mean and mean what you say. It starts in the NOW.

I AM is the statement that we begin with, as in when Hamlet says, "This is I, Hamlet the Dane." In the text of the play it means he is claiming his kingship and the identity he was borne to fulfill. In the realm of the work of this book, it is the model for not waiting, wishing, or putting off "what we may BE."

If you are to BE a successful salesperson, for example, then it is time to start BEING it in every possible moment. The statement is not I WILL be successful; the statement is I AM successful. Come to that conclusion with strong conviction, and you will wear that new future like a new suit of custom-tailored clothes. Your wearing an *actual* new suit informs how you feel, act, and carry yourself, and that is just a bunch of swatches of material sewn into a pattern. Imagine how powerful it feels if you "put on a new suit" on how you think!

What I am today is a result of who I was yesterday, and what I *may be* is a result of who I am today.

What We Are Exercise:

Write out a simple paragraph of who you are right now—facts mostly.

Now add about 10 percent "embellishment" to it. For example, if you're a salesperson, then make yourself a team leader/manager. If you're already a team leader or manager, then make yourself a vice president, etc.

Embellish another 10 percent. Now instead of VP you're a senior executive VP with stock options and your salary has increased 20 to 50 percent.

Now add another 10 percent to that and stop there.

Now take that stopping point, whatever the details as they are in your final embellishment, and put it on the top of a page. Working from that final embellishment, write down all the things that would have to happen to make that picture of your future self come true.

It might look like this:

Goal: Senior VP of Sales, North America
Triple my sales numbers now, which means building my network bigger
I'd need more strategic alliances
I'd need to do a weekend MBA course (would the company pay for it?)
Talk to HR head to ask what I need to do to get my next promotion: when?
Take time management course so that I don't neglect family while pursuing this
Get in better physical shape to keep me sharp and healthy, with a good attitude
Start dressing for success—check in with wife's image consultant friend
Investigate hiring a coach for growth
Re-write resume to see what else is out there in case I get stalled here
Etc, etc, etc.

All of the elements I've listed are pretty generic. Use mine as a starting place or guide if you'd like, but flesh out as many of the details as you can for your specific instance. You may take one look at the list and decide it's not what you want after all; that's ok too. If you find your are willing to do it all, but it's not likely to happen in your current circumstance then prepare your 'exit plan'.

Now go get busy taking on as many of the things on the list as you can, as soon as you can. Today's the day, after all; today's the day!

When sorrows come, they come not single spies, but in battalions.

Hamlet, Act IV, Scene 5

Brace yourself; it's going to be a bumpy ride. But the good news is that you can steer.

"Bad things come in threes"; ever heard that? Well, it's not really true as much as once something "bad" happens we are weakened, vulnerable, and can slip into the "victim" that waits in the wings for all of us.

G-d forbid something goes wrong: with your health or that of a family member; with your job or finances; with your relationship or any other "safety zone" in your life. You adjust your pattern to create a way of dealing with whatever happened, and you channel your energy into this "recovery." Then, when you are not at the top of your game, you have to deal with something else, and in your weakened state you create the idea that "Oh, no, it is a pattern!"

Listen, no one has ever been able to prove that "bad things" are clumped into groupings or patterns or that they can be attracted by one incident of "bad luck" or a breakdown. We may WANT to believe it so that we don't have to face the facts as they are, but it is just a natural occurrence; the quicker you deal with each and every incident as its own individual occurrence, the better for everyone.

Life is great because we choose to see it that way. What choice would you make? But does that mean that no one will ever get sick, die, have an accident, etc? NO. It means only that when these things do inevitably happen, that you can have your reaction to them, live that moment of your life as G-d and the universe intended, and get on with what's next. Who knows? No one knows, ever!

Sorrows in Battalions Exercise:

Create a list of "islands of safety" in your life.

For example:

> "My <u>marriage</u> is solid, and I love and trust my partner. We sometimes fight, want to get better at communicating, etc. like all human beings, but underneath it all we're a solid couple."
>
> "My <u>kids</u> are great." I'm proud of my kids and know they're growing up right.
>
> <u>Job</u>: no job is ever 100 percent assured, but right now I'm having good results and have a strong relationship with my co-workers and boss.

Continue the list, creating all of the "islands of safety" that you can.

Wherever your real "troubles" or "ills" are right now, put them on an island too. For example, if your home finances are where your troubles are coming from, then first create the island of safety that <u>you have a home</u>, that <u>you're able to cover (what percent?) of your expenses</u> etc. and then see how much is lacking for this to be a bona fide island of safety.

> Your next focus will be on the areas that are really not working and making that aspect of your life another island of safety.

For those "troubles" that you can't do anything about: Forget them! I mean, if, for example you hear that three of your friends have illnesses, well what can you do about that anyway? I don't mean to be careless or mean-spirited here, but what are *you* worrying about in such an example? Stop worrying and do something nice or kind for them and stop focusing on your fears and imaginations more than the good you can do for others!

Can you see what a waste of time it is to try to link all of the troubles into a myth? Come on: life is short, baby! Get moving and stay focused!

Cut the drama, mama!

Fair judgement, without the which
we are pictures or mere beasts.
Hamlet, Act IV, Scene 5

Every choice is ours to make.

YOU made the choice; don't try to pass it off to the moment, circumstance, a passing weakness, etc. It was a choice, and you made it.

If the choice happened while you were in a lessened capacity, like being drunk or stoned, well, you made the choice to allow yourself to be in that condition in the first place.

If the choice happened in an intense emotional or physical moment and you gave in to your sexual urges, well at some point you saw it coming and should have got the hell out of that situation.

We can and do act as beasts at times, however, by allowing our corporeal and carnal natures to lead us. Ok, so what? So we can use it for the energy it provides or be used *by* it. One choice works to add to life, the other to attach a weight of guilt that gets carried for too long no matter how clear you become or how much work you do on yourself.

And if you do give in to the beast, then forgive yourself and get on with it. It is NOT just more proof of any bestial self you may claim, just a mistake, plain and simple. Keep moving towards the best of you, the best in you, and the best you are meant to be: YOU as pure BEING.

Pictures or Mere Beasts Exercise:

Read this short section over and then do exactly this: Rip this page out of this book and crumple it into a wad. Throw it on the floor or burn it.

How's that feel? Notice the world falling down? Anyone around you bleeding or screaming? People may be looking at you funny—"Who rips books, I mean, what the ...?"—but no one died. Listen, a little rule-breaking feels fun sometimes. It's a choice, not a life sentence!

Rip. Crumple. Throw. RRRRRoarrrrrrrrrrrrrrrrrrrr!

This Page Intentionally Left Blank.

Love is begun by time, and that I see,
in passages of proof, time qualifies
the spark and fire of it.

Hamlet, Act IV, Scene 7

Keep love alive.

Forever.

How?

Who knows?

If familiarity does, indeed, breed contempt, then each relationship must be doomed with each passing day. What is funny and cute when we start out becomes trite and sad with time. Can it be that we were wrong when we met this new person, that he or she really IS different after we've known the person awhile? Not really; what has happened is we've failed to regenerate our love and affection. This affects not only lovers, boyfriends, girlfriends, husbands, and wives but family, our jobs, and just about anything we have in our lives for a span of time.

The clue or cure, the secret or function to draw on, is contained in the statement by Marcel Proust: "The real act of discovery lies not in finding new lands but in seeing with new eyes." Accept 100 percent responsibility for keeping the relationship or environment fresh and do the work that's necessary. Work? Should a true and lasting relationship require work? If you are asking that question, you are either new to relationships or extremely unenlightened. Every fire, no matter how hot, needs to be stoked and fed in order to keep burning.

One method to use to achieve "keeping it hot" is to stop and look at the way you listen to your "other(s)." Make sure you are not stuck in knowing what they'll say next, even when you do. Step outside of yourself and judge if you are listening FOR, ABOUT, or TO. Listening FOR is waiting for what you have mentally predicted them to say. It can also be waiting for them to say something with which you can "build your case" to compete or correct them with. If you are listening

ABOUT, you are fast forwarding mentally to the "good parts" or "aurally skimming." Listening TO is an effort for most of us as it is rare that our minds are relaxed, open, and not subject to distraction. We listen well to professors we respect, luminaries in our lives, and anyone we have bestowed that filter on, but the truth is, even Einstein snored and had to be reminded to wash the dishes from time to time.

Passages of Proof Exercise:

Try this approach to listening and see if you can listen "to" more often. Use it for two full weeks and see what changes come about in your life.

In a meeting or negotiation, at home or at work, check out the body posture of whomever you're with. In that very moment, notice how people are holding their hands, or crossing their arms or sitting a little forward in their chair, etc. Try subtly copying the "gist" of their posture so that you look like a conceptual mirror to them, but not so obviously that they notice what you're doing. Just being "in their bodies" a bit will give you a little more empathy for their positions and will give you a subconscious connection to them. Not only will you hear them better, but they will *feel* that you are "on the same page" with them. The technique needs to be handled subtly and tactfully, and I've hardly explained the full range of the concept, but if you try it for a while you will be surprised with the results.

This exercise, by the way, is a simple expansion of some physical acting exercises, in particular "The Mirror Game." I had a lot of luck with this one in finding new physicality to portray characters and to open up a "collective consciousness" in my classes in the past; people would sometimes be able to successfully do the mirror game with a partner in short bursts with their eyes closed! There are also some technologies that go even further on this point, like Neuro-Linguistic Programming. I leave it up to you if you want to research it and do more training and work on it. I am not recommending any particular group or process; just do the research on what's out there and make your best choice if you follow through on this. Good luck.

That we would do we should do when we would. For this "would" changes and hath abatements and delays as many as there are tongues, are hands, are accidents. And then this "should" is like a spendthrift sigh, that hurts by easing.

Hamlet, Act IV, Scene 7

Cut out *should, would,* and *could*; they're excuses, lies or, at best, band-aids to the real facts.

Judgments at best are you telling other people how *you* would live *their* lives if they were you. Actually it is you telling people how you would live their lives *if you were who YOU think you are or should be* and in "a perfect world." Well, there is no perfect world (although good French Roast and the *International Herald* at a corner bistro in Paris is darn close to perfect).

Be forgiving of others and the choices they make, because that's all we have: choices. At each and every moment we try to do our best; no matter how strong or weak we are at the moment, we do the best we can *at the moment*. It is too late to help AFTER the choice has been made and the action taken. You "should" have done this or that is a version of "I told you so." The place you need to be is in someone's life BEFORE he or she makes the wrong choice.

Speaking your mind is actually standing for someone and telling him or her the truth whether he or she will like it or not. Just remember that we are all human, and ever since the first couple lived in a perfect world, we've been good people who sometimes make bad choices.

YOU don't get to judge, "lest ye be judged."

Should is Like a Spendthrift Exercise:

We'll need three sheets of paper, held landscape style (sideways).

Each page should be labeled one of the following: Should, Would, Could

On each page put a center line.

On the left side of each respective page write down everything, and I mean everything, that should, would, or could happen. Have some fun with this one because it is your chance to RIGHT THE ENTIRE WORLD. Take your time, and on the appropriate page write your list and make it as long as you can, using only the left hand column. Add things you should do, specific people in the world should do, the world in general should do, the government should do, etc.

I'm doing my own list right now, too, so go ahead and make your pages. I'll come back when I'm done, and we'll move on.

Finished? Not yet? Well, let's just work with what you've got. It could be a long list, and we want to move ahead.

Now that you have at least three pages, each with a title of Would, Should, or Could, and a line down the center, start filling in the right side of the page with what you're going to do about each item. Ok, BREATHE, take it easy; there's a solution here.

> Some of the things on these lists you're already doing something about. Write that down, and if you want to "up the ante" on any of them do that.
> Some of the things on the list will be marked "don't feel like doing anything about it right now." Be honest; that's ok.
> Some will be marked "Later. Much, much, later."
> Some will be marked: "What was I thinking!'
> Some—well, it's up to you what to mark the others.

What this exercise can do for you is to break the habit of being a complainer, grouser, or defeatist and either diffuse that wasted energy of always finding what's lacking in the world or get you in action to create a better world, a solution, and a plan. If not you, who?

Good luck!

By the way, you really SHOULD share this exercise with friends!

If I COULD, I WOULD.

This project should have a back or second, that might hold if this did blast in proof.
Hamlet, Act IV, Scene 7

Always have a "plan B"—and don't need it.

If you are declaring that a thing will be, then declare the result and what the accomplishment will look like. Details are unnecessary at this stage of the game and can, in fact, be a "back door" and a way to get out of your commitment.

For example, in working with a sales team, I have the team members say, "I will sell a million dollars in business this week." I don't let them say "if, then, when," etc. because then they tend to tie the result to the predictable events already in place. They mean that "if" a certain contract gets returned on time, "then" they will get an order for business and "when" the client makes their decision, etc.

What I ask them to do is to **commit to the result** and then have it happen; even if they have to go to plan b, plan c, or plan z. Don't get stopped or beaten by what you were predicting and the effect that other people living in their own worlds, being affected by their own circumstances, might throw at them.

Say "this will happen" not "this will happen if …," and don't sell out your first plan by getting stopped too easily either. Keep asking what it would take to "make this happen" and keep moving forward. Get anyone you deal with to be a partner in you winning the game you are playing. People like to cheer a winner on.

Blast in Proof Exercise:

Take every event that you can foresee for the next twelve months and put them on a list on a piece of paper. Write every day off that's already scheduled (Labor Day, July Fourth, Bastille Day, etc.). Project your vacation days; even if they're not scheduled, use your best guess and put them in the schedule. Write all your religious or spiritual days of observance. Write your haircuts; needs for new clothes (how many shirts do you buy in a year? Underwear, socks, etc.). Write down everything that you know already that is in your life or that you want to be in your life this year: exercise, reading, art, learning, etc.

Now take a calendar, or print out twelve individual months from your computer. Fill in all of the events from the sheet of paper onto actual dates in the calendar. This is an exercise, so don't over-think it. Sometimes you'll have to arbitrarily put things on a date just to have a place to keep them. For instance, buying shoes is not something you'd normally schedule in advance, but for this exercise you'll figure that each year you buy two pairs of slippers, shoes, or sandals and actually put them as an item on a day in your calendar. This takes a bit of time but have patience.

Do you see how many things are already in your life? You may not necessarily plan them, but you do them all the same. Now suppose you got used to this idea of having a year's "plan"? Would it help you feel connected to your "author-ship" of your life? And, if it works for the small and predictable things ...

Now take on the "iffy" items like whether your vacation is in Mexico or at the local flea market buying terra cotta pots and colorful blankets. Using any of the other techniques learned from this book or just simply working backwards, plan and strategize whether or not you'll get your dream vacation or just the dream. *If you can fully commit to having it happen, then do what it takes to have it.* Or, if you can't create a compelling vision for the vacation, get real and create the plan for the vacation you're really committed to. Get real and get moving. Make it happen, ok?

PS—I do a version of this exercise around the first of the year with my clients; I prefer it to any of those New Year's Resolutions thingies. It is a great way to really get what is important to you, what you're already committed to, and to being responsible for what is in your life now and to come. Filter the things you're committed to through the values you hold dear and the qualities of life you want to achieve. Make it count as well as make it real.

I have a speech of fire that fain would blaze, but that this folly drowns it.

Hamlet, Act IV, Scene 7

Yelling doesn't solve anything or …

Shut it. Zip. Stop.

We've heard wonderful, impassioned, world-changing speeches from the Reverend Martin Luther King, Mahatma Gandhi, Winston Churchill, John F. Kennedy, Helen Keller, the Dalai Lama, and others, but do you think they made them up on the spot?

In any situation that you can imagine, your yelling, your righteous indignity, your "speech-ifying" will not have anywhere near the power of some good, solid, active listening.

I promise you that your wanting to talk, your wanting to be heard, your NEEDing to have your say, is your ego at work. You want to get the "stroke," you want to tell your fabulous story, you want to make sure you are in control of the situation, you want, you want, you want, cluck, cluck, cluck. Did I mention that the words "want" and "lack" were interchangeable in Shakespeare's time? You LACK when you cluck.

You will change more minds by creating trust while you listen. More often than not the required response to any question, if unguarded, un-defensive, and truly honest, is as short as one word or a few: "yes," "no," "I hear you," "I'm interested," "You matter."

Listen and let in.

You can hear the world changing.

Speech of Fire Exercise:

Find a <u>Toastmasters Club</u> near you. An Internet search will usually be sufficient, and you'll be surprised how many there are in any given metropolitan area. Schedule observation visits to a few of them over a few weeks as a guest. Don't just sit there, though. Notice how efficiently they run their meetings, the structure of each event, their respect for words and phrases, and the courage of the people embracing one of humanity's top fears: speaking in public. You will be humbled by their sincerity, I promise you, and you may just learn something about organizing your thoughts.

Step 2:

There are several books out there of the world's greatest speeches; Churchill, Gandhi, Kennedy, King. Get them and read them. Get some on CD if you can and listen to them. You can become inspired by words alone, can't you? Now if you matched the passion of your own words to the commitment of action ...

Oh, for a muse of fire! Ok, ok, I know: different play.

Cudgel thy brains no more about it, for your dull ass will not mend his pace with beating.

Hamlet, Act V, Scene 1

Sometimes the answer to the hardest problem is to let go of the *effort* of finding the "right answer."

Did you ever try hard to remember someone's name and then you can't, for the life of you, bring it to the front of your brain? You can't remember it although you say it is on "the tip of your tongue." The solution, for most everyone, has always been to beat yourself up, try, try, try and struggle, struggle, struggle, effort, effort, effort, blah, blah, blah …

Again I say it, *get out of your head*; it is a dark place with little light— unless you are suffering from a severe head wound!

Breathe. Let go. Trust. Breathe and breathe again. Ask G-d for the answer, meditate, pray, go for a walk, laugh, whittle, do a little ball bouncing off a wall or any other thing that can take your mind "off of it" (anyone ever tell you to "get off it"?).

Your mind, thought brilliant, can only do so much—and it was only intended to do so much. Figuring the tip at a restaurant: trust your brain. Want to know the "right thing to do": give your brain the day off.

Your Dull Ass Exercise:

Stop Thinking.

I mean it; just stop thinking. Let's allow some time for your "active" brain to relax and access some other parts of that complex gray matter.

Get out a big piece of paper and take a pencil in hand. Without looking down at the paper start tracing a drawing of whatever you're looking at. Just keep your hand from leaving the page so that you're drawing continuously so you won't be tempted to look down at your "art." Keep going until you feel you're done but don't rush it. Just take your time.

Try this exercise a few times over and take your time.

A variation is that you can try sketching scenes, things in the room, furnishings, etc. as best you can. About half way through, switch hands and draw with your non-dominant hand.

It's not about the finished product, by the way; it's about letting yourself relax a bit and being "out of your brain" for a while.

Add some of the things we've mentioned just previously:
> Walks in nature
> Exercise
> Whittling
> Mindless repetitive motions like bouncing a ball against a wall.

Just take the time to get out of that dark, cramped space where you THINK your identity lives and touch base with the *impulse of you*.

No further "point" to this exercise—that would just satisfy your "brain" addiction. Relax. Breathe. Breathe. Relax.

We must speak by the card, or equivocation will undo us.

Hamlet Act 5, Scene 1

Make it real, or it will make you false.

Take anything, any thing you say you want in your life—and by that I mean a quality or a task, an event or an experience—and make it REAL. "By the card" means that you put whatever you intend into some sort of existence system (like a calendar) and then you keep your appointment with yourself. This may sound simple, but it is really a big issue for most all humans. Why? Because we're HUMANS!

I don't mean to utilize this for only the easy stuff either, like announcing the date of your housewarming party so that you are forced to unpack, make design choices, and not live out of cartons until you decide what to do in your new place (though that is a good one). I'm talking more about the lies we tell ourselves when faced with the discipline of doing what we said we would do in the face of anything that "comes up."

Live by the card; write down what you will do and when and then actually have it happen. It's not as easy as it seems. If you need help, get coaches or nags, sponsors or benefactors, mentors or bullies, but get help. For me, I wrote this book in fits and starts until I enlisted Rosie and Cliff, two angels in my life, who weekly called me and asked me if I wrote my scheduled number of pages on the calendar. I had pre-wired them that I might (darn probably) make excuses, rationalize, or say "I didn't feel like it" and that they should admit no "BS" from me. One of them was willing to let me "off the hook" more readily than the other sometimes, but they both did what I asked. They provided the "outside eye" that kept me honest with my own self. That you are reading this now is a testimony to their "living by the card" so that I might not be undone by my own "equivocating" spirit. (Thank you, both, and bless you forever, Rosie and Cliff.)

Meet it is I set it down—schedule it, and then make it happen, ok?

Speak by the Card Exercise:

Can we chat for a moment? I want to acknowledge that we do a lot of exercises of this type in this book. If you're up to creating a life of your dreams instead of a dream of a life, you need to get in relationship with your word and having things happen because you say so. With that said, I try to make each on a little different, and I hope you try them all. There's a big pay-off here, and a lot of the work I'm doing personally around these "say do, do so" exercises just keeps getting deeper and deeper. Thanks for letting me chat with you; let's move on.

Take a look at your "Hundred Things to Do Before You Die" list from "We Fat All Creatures Else to Fat Us ..."

Pick one item that is a low- to medium-difficulty accomplishment. Create a plan, using any method you've learned in this book or that you've been using before this book, but it has to include weekly components and a timeline for completion.

Tell three to five friends about what you're up to and ask them to be your "angels." That means that you will share your timeline for the project and your weekly goals, and you will ask them to be your nags, your conscience, your accountability police, whatever you want to call it. I say ask three to five because you need at least two people and it's a big responsibility that some people might say "no" to.

Journal about your reactions to their support and how it makes you feel, but don't confuse their help with your fears, "stuff," anger, or reluctance to complete the task no matter what gets in the way. When you're done, check off your list and celebrate!

Don't forget to say "thank you" to your angels and give them some sort of sincere and appropriate gift.

This is I, Hamlet the Dane.
Hamlet, Act V, Scene 1

Be your name.

This scene in the play *Hamlet* is the turning point of the whole play, yet some productions don't even address it. Hamlet has just survived a plot to murder him and an adventure at sea. People who know him well don't recognize him in his new resolve, and when asked who he is, he answers with the phrase above. The phrase means not only is he claiming to be of right mind, but it uses the phrase "The Dane" as in "The KING" of Denmark, the role stolen from him by his fratricidal uncle. From this point on in the play, Hamlet no longer acts "crazy" nor is he "melancholic" or undecided. This moment is when he finally decides to take action, no matter what the consequence.

Have you ever done something that surprised people or displayed an unusual passion for something and had someone say, "Who are YOU?" The person is not recognizing you as you normally are, and many times you may even surprise yourself. You are claiming a new you, and then all you have to do is sustain it (simple, yet not easy). You see, many times we feel we have to know how to go about anything in order to achieve it, and that is patently untrue. The first step is in saying WHAT will happen or WHO you intend to be. Figuring out HOW is a moment-to-moment thing.

"Be your NAME" as Dr. Seuss says in *Oh the Places You'll Go* (read this book immediately).

So…

> be your name Buxbaum or Bixby or Bray
> or Mordecai Ali Van Allen O'Shea,
> you're off to Great Places!
> Today is your day!

This is I Exercise:

Get a mirror. A big one. Get a chair—not too comfy, just enough.

Sit in front of the mirror and stare. That's it. Stare. Let anything that happens, happen. If you want to laugh, laugh. If you want to cry, cry. Five minutes is the minimum time for the exercise, but twenty would be better.

Bonus points: Do the exercise standing naked before the mirror.

Journal about what you see, feel, and experience.

Take time with this one.

I am not splenitive and rash,
yet have I in me something dangerous.
Hamlet, Act V, Scene 1

We all have our "prisoner" inside.

How often we let our prisoner out is up to us, and whether we see it as "good or bad" is up to us too. I see it as good to have something "dangerous" inside of us that we can draw on when we need.

The key is to tap into that "something dangerous" side and draw on that well of energy to move yourself ahead powerfully. Now if you went and grabbed a live power line, you'd be blown into your next life. The same is true for this—if you tried to grab hold of this energy without "grounding" yourself, you could wind up getting hurt or hurting someone else.

Splenitive and Rash Exercise:

We're going to write some letters, so get out some paper; don't worry about how fancy it is because no one will ever see it except for you. At the top of the page, address the letter to whom or what you have some "energy" around and then begin the letter with "F*CK YOU." Then just let go.

Oops, I might have lost some of you for the reason that *this is strong language.* So do what you're comfortable with to get started (like abbreviating it to FU), but in truth, to really appreciate the catharsis and freedom this exercise provides it works best if you allow yourself to draw on your "dark side" and spell the whole word out as it would appear on a public restroom wall. Then just write, write, write, without over-thinking it, making it hard, or censoring yourself. It doesn't need to make sense either, like *writing the letter to an old bicycle and blaming it for disappointing you when you were five years old;* all that matters is that if it comes to you, let it flow.

Write as many letters to as many aspects of your life as you can think of: your job, your parents, your spouse or partner, your neighbor, highway drivers, money, your body, greed, envy, etc. *In one group I was leading one participant got right down to it and wrote his first F*CK YOU letter to himself.* Everyone should write that one, but don't worry about the order, priority, or if it makes sense. If it pops into your mind, write a letter to it. Don't worry about how long the letters are, but do try to keep it to one topic at a time.

Remember that we are purposefully drawing on your dark side for this exercise, so go ahead and let it all out. If you think you don't have any "F*CK YOU"s in you for anyone or anything, then get coaching, talk to a friend, or just fake it. Sorry to push back, but if you don't have a "F*CK YOU" in there for anyone, then you really are being a big "F*CK YOU" to the world without even knowing it, and that is dangerous.

Once you've written three or more of these you'll find a sense of release, freedom, and new energy coming to you. The more you write, the better you'll feel. The goal is to empty out that cesspool of undelivered anger and to do it responsibly. Resist the urge to go and deliver the contents of the letters directly to anyone; there is another exercise like that for later. Right now all you need to do is to tap into that energy flow and get "even." The next time you come face to face with someone from one of the letters, you can be straightforward and honest with him or her; you'll never have to hold back again. And you will have a new sense of energy and freedom that will leave people unable to say "no" to you!

Let Hercules himself do what he may,
the cat will mew, and the dog will have his day.
Hamlet, Act V, Scene 1

Practice non-attachment.

Do you ever get it that what is happening is what is happening and that no matter what you do to resist or fight it, you can't change that? G-d bless you if you can be ok with "what is," because so many of us don't on so many levels and on so many occasions.

In conversation:

> Person 1: "It's hard to get motivated today because it's raining."
> Person 2: "Oh really, because it's perfectly dry where I am."

What is the point of that response?

Or in planning;

> Person 1: "I can't make it tonight; my baby sitter just called, and she has the mumps and there's no back-up."
> Person 2: "But you SAID you'd come over today."

So your statement will cure the babysitter's mumps?

The weather:

> "It's so cold outside"
> "But the weatherman said it would be warm …"

Randomly:

> "This is not supposed to be happening …"

You see a pattern here, don't you? Can you admit that we're all prone to this at one time or another? We want things *to be the way we want them to be*, the way we need them to be, the right way, right? Well, as I've said here before, you can be happy or you can be right, and it is seldom the same thing. In fact, being at peace is the gift of being ok with not being right even when you're right (see "What do you read, my lord?") so I won't explain it again.

In fact, in order to be brief, as "brevity is the soul of wit," let's use an example.

Two cars occupying the same lane at the same time equals a dented fender. At that point, does it matter that one person is *right* or *wrong*? Does pointing the finger, yelling, and calling the other person a "stupid head" make the dent disappear? Of course it doesn't, yet we try that tactic over and over. Neither does it work knowing what the other person could have said or done, knowing what is right or fair, knowing what the Bible says, knowing what "they say," etc. What is happening is what is happening, and you must first "get it" in order to "be with it," in order to truly get that the world is a randomly occurring field of all possibilities and we are along for the ride.

That is not to say you should be resigned or disheartened; just don't waste too much time trying to fit what is happening into your "should." The more times you "should" on someone, the less happy you will wind up being with yourself, others, and the world around you.

Cat Will Mew Exercise:

Pick someone from your past who has wronged you, the most recent event that you can think of. Either you were wronged, or you "lost" and someone else won. Try to reenact the incident in your mind exactly as the facts occurred. Check that last phrase out: *exactly as the facts occurred.* Remember that your filter will want to reenact the story with you as the "winner," the one "in the right." Spell out the whole thing as much as you can, as impartially as you can.

Now go back over the story and make the other person right or make the "win" be deserved. Make the story come out authentically in favor of your "antagonist" even if it's the phone company or some other bureaucratic dead end.

The next step is to write a sincere letter of apology to the other person, persons, utility, or government agency. Write the apology completely and sincerely from the stance that you were wrong, you were "guilty" and/or mistaken. You never have to send the letter, by the way; the writing of it is enough.

Do as many instances as you want. Keep track of what opens up for you in your journal. You may wind up actually seeing how you might have handled the situation in a different way or learn a new level of patience.

Good luck!

There's a divinity that shapes our ends.

Hamlet, Act V, Scene 2

Do we really have any say in our destiny?

How do you handle the concept of an all-powerful, all-knowing G-d, or a space/time continuum in which past, present, and future all are already present, a fate you are living into, and the concept of "choice"? Well, one way to deal with it is you find some things you know for certain that you like to do, that give pleasure or fulfillment, and you do them as often as possible and wise.

Ok, maybe that's how I handle it, and maybe you are different.

So there is a divinity that shapes our ends, we are moving toward the purpose for which we were put here, and it is no surprise to G-d, yet we have a choice? Bullocks, eh?

Try this: all of the conceptions of fate/destiny/purpose and the ends being in the beginnings are true, it all matters, and right here and right now we are creating and recreating the world. We are the shapers of destiny and the victims of it as well, and it is the same as buying a ticket for a thrill ride that you know for certain won't crash. You ride in fear as if it will crash— and you paid handsomely, waited on a long ride, and went out of your way to do it. You bought your ticket, you take your chances.

G-d, or the Universe, has given us a form, an energy, and a key to the car. We head toward our destination but find all of these really interesting roads, detours, and stops along the way. We are always, generally, heading towards where we need to end up, but we don't have to keep on a straight line, hardly varying from course as if we were on train rails, or being a simple passenger looking at life through the windows as it passes by.

No, we are the ones deciding what is up ahead, creating the diversions, the side roads, and side trips with a turn of the wheel at every intersection, and when the road is straight, we still are making constant, tiny corrections to our steering as we go. We could pull off the road at any time and our destination would then come to us, but why not squeeze every mile out of this old heap while we can?

Life is not about finding oneself, as the sign on my desk reads, it is about creating oneself. Where will YOU point the vehicle today so that you enjoy the ride more than you did yesterday or the day before that? Get to it now, because I can guarantee there are some detours and roadblocks coming, and they will need to be addressed.

Choose.

Here's a fun story: A poor man works hard and one day finds himself enjoying a hard-earned wealth beyond his wildest childhood fantasies. He has a beautiful home, a beautiful wife, and a stable of the fastest horses in the world. One day he is walking in the market in Tel Aviv, and he sees the Angel of Death. The Angel of Death also sees him, looks quickly at him, and begins to raise his skeletal hand towards the man. Quickly the man flees the market, goes home and explains all to his wife, takes two of his fastest horses, and flees the Angel of Death, going to Jerusalem where he will hide in a shop his father-in-law owns.

After he has safely fled, his wife heads for the market looking for the Angel of Death. Finding Death she is more irate than scared, and she admonishes him: "Why did you scare my husband so and then not even finish what you started? That is cruel beyond belief!"

"You must pardon me," said Death. "I was just surprised to think a mistake had been made. Here I see your husband wandering aimlessly among the stalls in this market, and yet I have an appointment to meet him far, far away tomorrow in a small shop in Jerusalem. How I could be so wrong …"

Divinity Shapes our Ends Exercise:

Get out some index cards and a magic marker, please.

Write on the index cards: "Yes," "No," "Hero," "Lover," "King," "Flee," "Wizard," "Ask for help," "Call Mom," "Challenge," "Say Thank You," "Acknowledge," "Go to a movie," "Ask what they need," "Ask an expert."

For the next two weeks, any time a challenge or problem comes up, shuffle the cards and do what it says on the card. For instance, if it comes up "Hero," imagine what a mythic hero would do in this case. If "Challenge" comes up, then you're being challenged and you need to find what the challenge is and take it on. Do your best interpreting and putting into action according to the cards without telling the whole world what you're up to. See how long you can pull this off.

The randomness of this exercise can actually springboard you into the next level of understanding the choices you make each day, the "crap shoot" that every decision actually is.

By the way, I should add a disclaimer here that I want you to use your good sense with this one. *Don't call me saying you got divorced because of a card or something crazy like that; that won't work.*

'Tis dangerous when the baser nature comes between the pass and fell incensed points of might opposites.

Hamlet, Act V, Scene 2

If you are to win, must someone else lose?

We played a game the other night in which the people in my course had to let go of their firmly held belief that in order to win, someone else must lose. It was a short exercise, and it was set up so that there was no way to "win" the game unless *all* of the participants won. They assumed that the game meant having "all the marbles." In the interest of time I eventually stopped the game and debriefed them; "Who said winning meant the others had to lose, that there could only be one winner?"

Unbeknownst to them, they were still in the exercise after the "game" ended as it included cataloguing and listening to their reactions to "not winning" the game. Each objected in his or her own way, and the complaints varied from accusing me of not explaining the context of the game well enough, my manipulating the rules, or that the wording of the rules was intended to purposely mislead, etc. Few of them got it at first that they were operating under ingrained assumptions, assumptions that over time had taken them over and were running all of their "games."

Our session that night was about our "programming," our world view and the way we'd been trained, over and over, in contexts that didn't necessarily serve us, yet ones we insist on holding onto as if they were our lives. In fact, they actually are our lives, our lives as we have come to view them through repetition and pattern. We have been brainwashed, and in fact we have done some of the brainwashing ourselves. We have wrongly identified ourselves with our roles and with our family, cultural, school, and other influences, and we are passionate about holding on to that whether it serves us or not.

And then there are our emotional "patterns." We human beings, all of us, naturally want to make life easier, *and* we want to live the fullest

179

life. All that creates is constant struggle. We want to learn from our mistakes in order to limit our suffering and pain, and that can mean not allowing ourselves to be hurt again today by what hurt us yesterday. We'll say "Uh, oh, this situation seems similar to one where I got hurt before so, on the chance that I'll get hurt again, I'm not allowing myself to be vulnerable," or some version of that conversation. Our baser nature is FEAR, security, safety, and most of all, comfort. That is the error we need to correct in ourselves, and it is no easy job.

Start now, that's all I can ask. Eventually, the "pattern breaking" muscle will become stronger and you'll be living in between the "points" of "passions" as your daily way of being. By the way, *that* will also be a pattern, a numbness, and a "brainwash" but of a whole new type.

When we get there we'll talk.

Baser Nature Exercise:

The goal is to do nothing today that you did yesterday. Of course you have to decide what things are "non negotiable": daily prayers, medication, eating, etc.

These non-negotiable items may be "safe," but let's find ways to vary them in some way.

Change where or when you say your prayers, eat different foods, with different people, in places you don't normally go to, or at least change your seat at the table Move your watch to the other wrist.

Wear clothes you haven't taken out of the closet in a long time.

Little by little start to notice the places where you've become unconscious, where practice had bred numbness, and where it had become easier to use yesterday as the template for today than to create each day as new, different and unique.

Keep it up.

The interim is mine;
and a man's life no more than to say "one."

Hamlet, Act V, Scene 2

Life's short, use it well.

So let's get right to ...

The interim exercise:

Write your own epitaph.

Write out your life in two versions:

as it *actually is now* in one version and
then go on to embellish your life as it would be "if."

Pick the version you most want to be true and make it happen by following true and committed actions. Do this by taking a calendar out, and let's just plan the next year of your life. A year seems like a long time, but it will seem shorter if you plan that it is your LAST year, the LAST year of your life.

Now think of what you would do in the last month of your life?

How about the second-to-last month of your life?

Now take it down to what you would be doing next week, tomorrow, today, or NOW if you knew that this was the last year you had.

If THAT doesn't get you going, you are already dead and just waiting for the funeral!

I am constant to my purposes.
Hamlet, Act V, Scene 2

Say so; make it so.

There is a quote I heard about a person living a "full life." What was meant by "full life" was that the person did each day what was intended to happen on that day. The same applies for you.

Each day you are intended take on certain tasks, certain "doings," and they are all available and possible for you. If you leave them undone they may never come around again. (*That's a good thing. If every time you left one thing undone it got added to the grand list of "things to do," then you would be facing a list that got bigger and bigger every day, more hopeless each day, until it became not believable even in an ocean full of hope*).

If you really are constant to your purposes, you will live a full life by saying "yes" all day to what is next and being fully present, alive, and accepting of the challenge—whatever it might be. Get to your "to do" list today and every day. Don't give yourself a moment to be "numb." Even in the moments where you rest, pause and allow peace to take over your "front of brain" activity; stay "in the moment." The moments of watching TV, for example, might be on the list the universe has created for you to get to that day. It's not all about taking out the garbage or building a house for the homeless; it's about breathing in, saying "yes" and "thank you" for moments one after the other. Slow down and say a prayer with every moment in how you approach that moment with full consciousness.

Live a full life in even the simplest of activities so that the more complex ones can be more fully realized too. It is YOUR life; live IN it.

Constant Purposes Exercise:

Keep a "day diary." Each thing you do as you go through the day, write it down in your diary. Don't worry that it's too minor or to slow to put in the journal. Do this for a couple of weeks. What do you notice? Are you "in" each moment? Seriously, you can find out anything from this diary, even that your life is never numb, is fully conscious, and alive. Don't go into this "question" with the answer, any answer. Being open is the best tool you can apply here. After two weeks, make any adjustments that you want, use other exercises from the book if you want, or make no adjustments. What you'll see is that just observing will give you the breakthrough you want. Relax. Breathe. Lean on me. Good luck.

We defy augury.

Hamlet Act V, Scene 2

Create your own future.

Trick question: does everyone grow up to be the person he or she was born to be? Answer: you were not "meant" to be anything. You are "to be," and that is it. "To be or not to be," eh? Well there is truth here in that it is more important to create your future than to live into one that is really just your past dragged into your future. Do you know what that means, or am I being too vague?

Let's put it this way: your mom is a doctor, your dad is a doctor, your twin brother or sister is a doctor, and do you know what that means your career must be? It means that your mom is a doctor, your dad is a doctor, and your twin brother or sister is a doctor. And you are whatever you create yourself to be.

How do you create yourself? You create the vision of yourself for yourself. You only need to know "what," not "how." You speak it out loud and often; everyone and anyone who can help you needs to hear you in order to find you faster. You take committed action towards your goal. You don't let yourself get stopped—ever.

Life is not about finding yourself; life is about creating yourself. Remember?

Augury Exercise:

Make a list of you as you have always wanted yourself to be in your heart, in your dreams. Take your time and create the picture as completely as possible. Now get out the yellow pages and find instructors, lessons, courses, classes, and experts on any topic or item on your list. Get on the phone and sign up, ask for an apprenticeship, make a deal, or whatever it takes to get your "life list" into your life.

You are the actions you take in your life. You are what you put your energy into and where you spend your time. If what you try to add into your life doesn't fit, then at least you've tried. You will KNOW the difference between what you thought you wanted and what you really wanted, between what you thought was right and what was actually right. You will be the "you" that you are.

Choose you as you are now so that you can clearly see the you to be. Be content, as the Buddhist philosophy says, but don't be complacent.

Keep growing; keep going. Make you; that's your job. Take your time; it's a big job.

There is a special providence in the fall of a sparrow.

Hamlet, Act V, Scene 2

Little things do count.

Today I saw two women at our office take out a shoebox and save a small bird that had flown into the window and fallen onto the ground stunned and hurt. Others stood over the bird and talked about what a shame it was, "poor little thing," etc. And then these two women actually got the shoebox, picked up the bird, and made sure it was ok.

Get it?

Get it.

Pick up the bird.

And by the way, there are a lot of "little birds" out there.

Sparrow Exercise:

I cover this in so many ways that I'm going to keep this exercise simple. For the next few days try out chivalry. Hold the door for others. Pull out a chair for someone else to sit. Offer your seat to someone who needs it. Let someone cut you in line. Say thank you to the guy at the tollbooth. Be polite. Journal your experiences and share it with others. That's all. Thank you.

If it be now, 'tis not to come.
If it be not to come, it will be now.
If it be not now, yet it will come.
The readiness is all.

Hamlet, Act V, Scene 2

Today's the day.

Do you know how the world gets changed?

Wait for it …

Waaaiiiiiiiiiiiiiiiiiitttttttttttt …

There, did you see it? Just then; just there; just now; just THIS moment, and the world changed. Now there is some fantastic work being written about the Future and the Past never being here. The Future is a creation of the Present, and the Past is just a wad of gum stuck to your spiritual soul slowing your forward motion, etc., etc., etc., and you can find a lot of things to read about all of this "tense" work.

I'm going to skip it for this one and not even go into as broad a category as "the present." The Present is like a parentheses around this moment in time, it is made up of choice after choice, and it does, yes, indeed it does, create the future of our dreams or our nightmares.

Let's get smaller and even more specific than the Present and just deal with the Now or, more accurately, the Right Now. I can't discuss it better than this story. I was in religious services the other day, and my seven-year-old son was with me. I was trying to give him attention and pray at the same time. I was getting ready to ask G-d for some things, it being a good time to do so, when I was overwhelmed with the love I felt for my son right at that moment. No, it wasn't exactly right *at* that moment, it was just my love for my son *in* the moment right there, time AND place. It is hard to explain this, but it wasn't about my love for him right then as if I noticed something new about him. It wasn't a collection of emotion since he was born nor triggered by what he was doing right then. It wasn't how he looked at that moment any future projection of how he will grow. It was none of any of those. It was just LOVE *of* him, and it existed out of time. How do I know?

Because I became very "present" to a door that was open somewhere, a joy that was accessible to me right then and there, and there was no time involved, no thought for the future and no words of description; it was more of a feeling that caused me an intense joy, a warmth, and a pleasure that wasn't limited to the physical.

The door to heaven had opened, and in that moment I prayed without words for my son and all that G-d intended for him and all that the world held for him, good or bad. It was probably an extremely brief moment, as intense as it was, and then I started to "crash"; the feeling started to go away. My past, my pain, got dredged up, and it began to steal the moment. I thought of how much pain I had to experience to learn what I've learned and how I grew so much because my father died when I was just a little older than my son is now. It was really suddenly about me not wanting to miss him growing up like my dad missed me. Correction: I missed my father growing up, and the struggle of the moment became focusing out and being in a NOW, fighting with the past and future who were both trying to fill up, as they say in the movie *Spinal Tap*, a "much needed void."

In short, as soon as I filled the space with my own ego again, it got too crowded to support that "window" in the universe and the door open to G-d. I "crashed" back to earth, but not without stealing a little bit of heaven.

The Readiness Exercise:

Stop what you're doing right now and find a place or people that you love. Without making a big deal of it just sit there and take them in. I don't mean sit there and *think really hard* about what it is about them that you love or that is special; in fact don't engage your brain at all. Just sit there and pay attention to them; breathe them in. Do this again and again. In fact, put it on your calendar with as much importance as any other task in your busy life. Just "be with" the people you love, the places you love, and have no agenda. Let what comes to you come to you with ease and have the experience. Go ahead; this book will wait. So will I.

But while I allowed myself to be a part of that
one single moment ...
Since no man knows of aught he leaves, what
is't to leave betimes. Let be.

Hamlet, Act V, Scene 2

Live in the moment ...

We are so worried about what might be, what may be, what could happen. This obsession gets so firmly in our way that we often get separated from the actual moment, the NOW that we are in. We are robbed of our joy in this moment. So many great minds have written so well on this topic of "now" that I'm just going straight to the exercise about letting go of worry and fear.

Betimes Exercise:

Make a list of all the things you are afraid might happen. Write all the things that could go wrong, all the ways you could screw up over the next four weeks.

Then take that list, put it somewhere, and set a reminder on your calendar to revisit the list in four weeks.

Take out this list four weeks later:

Did any of your fears come true? If they did, was the consequence as dire as you imagined it? Did the worst REALLY come true? Be honest: what was the consequence to you?

Now look at all of the fears that didn't come true.

Get the message?

And "no," the fears you are facing today, now, in the next four weeks are not any different than the ones on the list you made four weeks ago, so don't try to fool yourself.

Let Be. Let Be. Get up to something and let your fears keep themselves company while you go out and enjoy each and every moment of this life you've been given. The good and the bad (*thinking makes them so*) will come and go in their time, but using your imagination to put them into an imagined future will only create stress and illness. Trust me, darlings: you don't need them.

Let my disclaiming from a purposed evil free
me so far in your most generous thoughts that
I have shot my arrow over the house and hurt
my brother.

Hamlet, Act V, Scene 2

Accidents happen. Forgive. But, then again …

We're back in *The Land of 100 Percent Responsibility*. Remember, please, that it is a make-believe world and that you have to suspend your disbelief in order to visit it. All it gives you is a place to stand and grow. It is not for the faint of heart; in fact you have to be a warrior to be there for more than a short time.

Each time you make a choice you bring about a consequence. If the consequence is that someone else gets hurt, then we are apt to "feel bad." But we are not our feelings. We are the results of the actions we take on top of the perfect beings we are created as. So how do we deal with pain, injury, and insult that comes to others through our efforts even if it is not our "fault"?

In *The Land of 100 Percent Responsibility* we may find ourselves making a decision or a choice that is the one we see as best. The consequence can be that someone we know will be disappointed or hurt, and this bothers us because **we like to be liked**. Your job, as a leader, as a person of integrity, is not to back down from doing the right thing because it might make you unpopular. Do what needs to be done and be a grown-up about it.

However, you can still live in *The Land of 100 Percent Responsibility* <u>and</u> create a compromise. Live out the consequence and then get in action for the person who feels he or she has been injured. Saying "sorry" is not for the other person; that is really just to make you feel better. Taking action means actually creating a service in that other person's honor. It could be "I know I chose another person for the job you asked me for, and I believe I made the right decision. I will offer to spend

195

time with you and create a plan that can move you closer to being in the right 'place' if this or another position comes around again. I will mentor you or find a mentor for you in order to give you every chance to grow and develop so that you are the first choice next time."

Please realize that the example I am citing above is oversimplified, and you, of course, believe it is nothing compared to the situation where you find yourself. In reality, it is not different. You are only making it seem that way, if you are, because you desire the drama. Cut that out.

It is this simple: if you hurt someone for any reason whatsoever and you want to make reparations, then DO something about it. Don't just *think* or *feel* with no thought of action or reaction, because that mental indulgence is just a back door and another way to wallow in the temptingly warm pool of your own ego. No ego pools in *The Land of 100 Percent Responsibility*. If you want to take a swim in this land, you've got to do it by diving in over your head—and LIKING it!

Hurt My Brother Exercise:

This one is simple. Make a list of everyone who you might have injured this year and contact each and every one of them asking for forgiveness. This is a request for forgiveness no matter how "right" you felt or justified in your actions. Let them know that at the time you were only doing your best and acknowledge that they paid a price. If appropriate, ask them if there is a way you could make it up to them in actions you might take.

The key here is that some people may say, "Forget you" and re-live the event as if it were occurring in the present moment, re-experiencing the emotions and pain like a replay of a soap opera. That is painful to observe, but there's nothing to be done about it; that work is theirs to do. You can only ask for forgiveness and offer restitution; if they refuse it, the matter is then between them and their G-d. You can leave the incident in the past and move forward without that extra baggage. Travel light in this land, my friends.

I do receive your offered love like love, and will not wrong it.

Hamlet, Act V, Scene 2

Accept apologies. Accept thanks. Accept praise. Accept what's given freely.

What's your response when someone tells you, "Good job," or "Thanks"? Can you manage a "You're welcome," or do you come up with some sort of deflection, making it hard for people to express praise or gratitude. Can you TAKE IT?

Well, here's what is happening. You're a fraud. At least you think so. You try and try to do more, win at whatever it is you want to win at, excel, exceed, and in general deserve praise. And then *Catch 22*-like when you earn praise and someone gives it to you, you can't accept it because you are, in your mind, a fraud. Who can win with you? No one can, least of all you.

You can spend a lot of time trying to find out why "you're not worthy," or you can just get in the habit of keeping your mouth shut for just a few seconds when someone says something nice to you. In those few seconds, short-circuit your usual "Well, it's really not me, it's my team's win," or the "I didn't really do anything" and just pause for a second. What if you just said thanks?

Would the person saying "Good job" all of sudden have a change of heart and think, "What an egotist—I gave him (or her) a compliment, and he (or she) just accepted it! As if I really meant what I said!" NO. The person would feel appreciated; he or she would have thrown a pass, and someone would have caught it. The person would have the feeling that he or she passed on some good feeling; if you can't do it for you, do it for him or her.

Why do so many of us think we're a fraud? Because we've witnessed ourselves as humans; we know that we have "bad" thoughts, doubts, fears, and that sometimes when we win it is a mix of luck, support, timing, and hard work supported by some *intangible* that just happened to fall into our path. Well, DUH! Do you know how many people are paying money to own a copy of the DVD or book *The Secret* to be told that we are all humans with doubts and fears and that we can create a win by applying committed action and thinking "forward-moving thoughts"? That if we apply our energy in the right way, intangibles and luck will come to support us?

Ok, *The Secret* has more to offer than that, but realize, if your intention is to have something happen and it happens, that you own a piece of that success. You only move all of us forward if you let that in and learn how to have it happen again and again, as often as possible.

Talk to the most successful people you know, and I say this with authority of having done so, and they will admit that they too often feel like a fraud. They feel that any day now someone will "find them out" and turn them in, as if there were an "authenticity police."

Do your best. Do it again. If someone likes it and has the need to say thank you, accept it from him or her. Do it for the other person if you need to; that's a good reason as any.

You are not a fraud, by the way; you are you doing exactly what you've chosen to do in exactly the way you're choosing to. And it is an active, every-moment thing, this deciding, and through it you earn everything you've got coming to you.

Give this "fraud" stuff up, no matter how much cause you have to doubt or hate yourself. Remember, every saint has a past, and every sinner a future. It all begins right NOW in this very moment. This one. This one. This one right here. NOW. Yes, NOW!

Accept Exercise:

This is not a journaling exercise; this is a practical exercise in the hopes that you'll create a new experience and practice.

Over the next week or so listen for people saying "Thank you" or "Good job" or any variation of those accolades. Your whole assignment is to be still in the moment, allow the "Thank you" or whatever to enter into your complex system of automatic reflexive/defensive responses, and just accept it. A proper response is "You're welcome," and any response longer than one to five words means you're not doing the exercise.

Let's role play:

> *Your boss: Thank you for staying late tonight to catch up this work.*
> *You: Oh, that's ok. I needed to catch up anyway so it's no big deal …*
>   *EEEEEEEEEEEEEE!*
> *(That's the "NO" buzzer going off—let's try again)*
> *Your boss: Thank you for staying late tonight to catch up this work.*
> *You: (Stop. Breathe. Be aware and let it in.) You're welcome.*

See how easy it is? Ok, it's simple, not necessarily easy, but I know you can do it. *Thank you for your willingness to take this exercise on.*

Your response is: _____

Added points if you extend this exercise by listening to other people who you are giving thanks or recognition to or who you might observe getting them from others. Notice their responses and how they handle it. Don't say anything to them; don't offer advice. Just notice and keep an open heart.

A hit, a very palpable hit.
A touch, a touch. I do confess it.
Hamlet, Act V, Scene 2

Celebrate your victories and your defeats.

We live most of our life on the plateau, working towards the goal. The goal itself only lasts for a moment as we experience the breakthrough, and then we're back on the plateau—the next one I'll admit, but a plateau all the same.

If you are working on getting your black belt in karate, playing a sonata, or even riding a bike for the first time, you have to work really hard to keep taking action towards the goal. Then the goal comes and you have this light bulb over your head, this seeming moment of the sun shining directly on you, etc., and then "nothing." You don't suddenly find yourself able to fly; instead you're just over the "hump" and looking at the top of the hill, only to find that there is yet another hill in the distance. So party on!

If you achieve something, stop and give yourself a pat on the back. Stop and reward yourself, accept praise from others, take a deep breath, and say, "Yeah, me!" Then go back into the studio, the dojo, the workshop and start working on the next goal with the patience of anyone pursuing mastery of life.

And if you try and fail, celebrate that too. If you work to be the number one sales person in your company and do the most and the best you can every single day, day after day, and you can honestly say "I did my best" when the results are published and you are number two or three instead of "top dog," then that too is a breakthrough. That moment of "ow" can be your moment of "wow," and you can make the choice whether to go back to basics and work on the next stage of the game or just say, "That wasn't my game" and find the next one. It's VERY difficult to ever know when it is the right thing to do—quit, resign, or move on—but it is a part of life just like anything else.

Remember it is a "hit" either way; it is a touch, and if you don't feel it then you're numb. NUMB is no way to live, to be live, to be A-live person—and that is why we're here, isn't it?

The **"Palpable Hit"** exercise is combined with the next topic, **"Best Violence."** Read on.

The proceeding section, by the way, was inspired in large part by a book you should read: Mastery, *by George Leonard. I don't claim to have created most of the ideas in this book nor am I accurately reflecting Mr. Leonard's wonderful ideas nor could I. Buy his book; go to the source.*

I pray you, pass with your best violence. I am afeard you make a wanton of me.

Hamlet, Act V, Scene 2

Don't play anyone small.

I will on occasion let my young children win a game; it depends on what they need to learn at the time. I won't let them win all the time, as it is important that they learn to both win AND lose.

Neither do I "cheat" anyone in my life and sell him or her short by condescending to him or her. I will let the person know the "game" we're playing by being direct and giving him or her a chance to "win." If it is an employee and I'm not getting what I want from him or her, I will make it very clear what is missing and get involved to create a win. Then it is up to the employee to do what is necessary and, with or without help, get done what needs to get done. If the employee chooses NOT to take action, then he or she has made a choice to play out and I feel no guilt in being a part of the employee moving on to the next part of his or her life.

You may think you're being "nice" to someone by not hurting his or her feelings or being too "rough" on him or her, but that is where the "play the wanton" comes in. You are really assuring that you will stay in control of the situation by always "knowing" (and by that I mean "believing") that *the other person* is wrong, less than you, weak, and incapable and that you have to protect him or her from something. That keeps you always in charge, always on top, and always "better than."

Look at masters of any sport for an example; they look for the competitors who will give them a real challenge.

Wanton and Palpable Hit combined Exercise:

Find someone with whom you share an interest—sports, hobby, career, or any shared passion or topic. Actually, find someone better at this interest than you or someone you think is better at it. Contact this person and ask him or her to spend time with you. If it is tennis, for example, contact a local tennis pro and ask him or her to join you on the court for a match—not lessons, at least not yet. Play opposite him or her so you feel what it's like to play a pro.

If it is business, write a letter to someone you admire in business, someone you see has the qualities and skills you admire. Invite the person to lunch or attend a seminar he or she is hosting or attending.

The particular of this is that you reach out and ask people who would clearly beat you in a match or competition and that you get comfortable with being around them, talking to them, or competing against them. Don't get lost in the "I suck" or "I'm no good" mire, either; just focus on them, their ease and grace at the task. Enjoy how they "win" or achieve and invite some of their spirit into you.

Now take a look at what you want for yourself in this particular avenue of your life and enroll someone else, a coach, a mentor, a teacher, or take a course, to give you a performance breakthrough. Play full out.

Play to do more than just win—play to grow past your previous bounds.

Why as a woodcock to my own springe, Osrick. I am justly killed with my own treachery.

Hamlet, Act V, Scene 2

What goes around comes around, sort of.

When does life begin to turn around for you? When is it that what you've been hoping for, waiting for, working for, etc. actually arrives? What gets in your way most of all—or should I say "who"?

I think you've got it by now: you can and, in fact, *may* be your own worst enemy. Here is what you can do for you in order to let yourself out of the trap you've laid for yourself: accept what is coming and get the concept that there is nothing wrong with you, nothing is wrong with you, and nothing is wrong with you.

G-d (or the Universe, etc.) is asking you to dance constantly, guiding you incessantly, and offering you joy and happiness or, at the least, peace. Each and every time we stop critiquing ourselves, second-guessing ourselves, and live in the next moment, we can relax into what is coming anyway. We have done the best we could, made the best decisions we could in each and every moment of our lives, and we deserve letting ourselves live in the peace of the "flow of the universe."

Here's a true story where I got a valuable lesson. A few years back I spent a week in a meditation "intensive." It was sixteen to eighteen hours a day of guided meditations, "process work," and I was repeating a fervent prayer that G-d would speak to me, directly into my ear, so that I would finally and actually hear the voice of G-d (very dramatic). On the fifth day of the six-day seminar, I suddenly started laughing spontaneously as I realized, once and for all, that G-d was, and indeed had been, talking to me constantly. My knack for cooking, my intuitive art making, my moments of joy in nature, the coaching I gave to my clients, riding bikes, being "dad," and all those moments where answers came without effort, when I experienced "*the flow,*" were all the voice of G-d. They were times when G-d was speaking very generously, very attentively, and very lovingly directly into my ear. Those moments have all been so prevalent in my life and I had been overlooking them for so long that to finally "get it" was the most freeing, emptying moment of that period of my life, and the doors opened for so much more. And it all came from "stopping" the "trying," from letting go of the trap I had created to hold me "safe."

But how will you put it? Let's try this: don't put it any way. Let it go. UN-trap your soul and your spirit. Osrick would want it that way.

Springes Exercise:

Let's make a "thank you" list.

Make a list of all the things you've completed or accomplished. This is different than a "Hundred Things to Do Before I Die" list and is almost like a "life resume/ curriculum vitae." Give yourself credit for everything you've done. List every medal you've ever won, every scout badge, certificate of achievement, etc. Make sure to include any diplomas, and don't take them for granted—high school, GED, all of them should go on the list.

This list includes staying married or in a relationship for a period of time. It includes staying at a job, reading this workbook, reading any book, making lunch for your school kids, raising kids, stopping smoking, or not biting your nails. Everything that you've done and accomplished with the time you've been given and the skills you innately have can go on the list. I'm not going to read it, so give yourself some room to enjoy this process.

Now read the list over to yourself and say "thank you" for the gifts you've received. What does this inspire you to accomplish? What, if you allowed yourself the natural gifts you've been blessed with, would you be "up to" next?

Keep the list nearby and refer to it from time to time. It can be your secret energy source and power you onwards. Thank you.

Things standing thus unknown, shall I leave behind me.

Act V, Scene 2

Live each day as your last; one day you'll be right.

This is the one I get "hot" about. Whenever I ask people about what they are passionate about or what they care for they usually have a long list of things that they say they stand for, are champions of, or that they were active with in college. My next question usually stops them dead: So when was the last time you actually were in ACTION on that? In the name of action, let's get right into the exercise.

Things Standing Exercise:

Make a list of all the things you think are important.

Make a list of things that need a champion in the world: feeding the hungry, ending poverty, saving the rainforest, housing for everyone, and a world of care and respect for all.

Get out your date book and make actual, RECURRING appointments to do something about any single one of them. Get it off your wish list and onto your to-do list, and do it now. Put this book down and do it.

Go ahead; I'll wait.

Done? Let's keep going.

Now invite five friends to also participate and make it so they can't say "no."

Do you see where I'm coming from? Get your desires for change and creating good in the world out of your head and into your fingers, toes, legs, lips, eyes, ears, and most importantly, into the world of the real. Make a difference by making a commitment and sticking to it. Things standing, thus undone, leave those that you could have helped unaffected and in pain. The world really does, as it turns out, need another hero; you're it.

Get to it now. I said "NOW"! (I told you this one makes me "hot.")

The rest is silence.
Hamlet, Act V, Scene 2

Breathe. Who knows what else there is?

Do you think you will "figure it out"? There is no power in the brain that could ever match what the universe, as one collective master teacher, is waiting to whisper in your ear. But you have so much noise going off in your head so often that it's hard to hear the instructions.

Michelangelo, when discussing the sculpture "David," said that the form and figure *were already there in the marble* before he began his work. All he had to do was to chip away the parts that *weren't* David. So it is with us; we all know all we need to know. We just get in our own way by trying to constantly fill the space with noise.

Need more proof? Sit in silence for even ten minutes a day for just a week. You may develop a habit of it.

The REST comes from silence, and the "rest"—and that means EVERYTHING available in the universe—is contained in the silence. Listen to the "no-thing."

Silence Exercise: ten to twenty minutes

Breathe.

Find a place where you can sit in quiet, where you can be undisturbed for ten or more minutes. Sit upright in a comfortable chair, but not one that's so comfortable that you'll fall asleep.

Sit and breathe.

Breathe in through your nose and, if possible, out through your nose.

Breathe.

Silence Exercise 2: As long as it takes

If you can manage to be aware while you're in the "heat of it," the next time you're feeling angry or tense, take a break, take a pause, and breathe. Breathe deeply and "listen" to your body. Listen for the areas that are the tensest. Once you notice a tightness or "hold," then breathe into that area and try to breathe out the tension. Give yourself permission to let go. Breathe. Breathe. You don't need to engage your brain on this one too much, just as a receptor for the signals the body wants to send. Breathe.

Flights of angels sing thee to thy rest.

Hamlet, Act V, Scene 2

Honor the dying and their journeys.

We are the ones who are sad when we lose a loved one. When faced with a loved one's passing, focus out, onto him or her. This person has pain to deal with on his or her own and doesn't need your fears, sadness, and grieving for YOUR sadness and fear of being alone, of not knowing how to deal with your emotions. Don't try to "understand" what the person is going through or give him or her advice—unless you yourself have died exactly the same way and have come back to tell him or her about it. Barring that circumstance, just shift your focus onto the person, what he or she needs and, short of words coming out of your head and mouth, reach out with your hand and just share that faint pulse from your hand to his or hers—that is communication from the heart.

Why should I include this quote—just because it is a beautiful image? Actually, I've done it wrong and done it right. My father died when I was eleven. Early on the day he died I visited him in his hospital room where he had wasted away from cancer. The moment I laid eyes on him I shot from the room in tears. Instead of giving him comfort, I needed comforting. He died hours later, and the last he saw of me was someone scared of him and how sick he looked. What do you want? I was eleven.

My mother, though, was nearing ninety and had lived a full life. I went to visit with her, and we just sat and talked—not about the old days or the good times; in fact I don't know what all we discussed. I was just there with her. Knowing the end was coming, the last time I left her hospital room she and I just smiled at each other, I said "So long" and "I love you," and she smiled at me just the way I would always want to remember her smile. A few days later, though she was unable to speak, I got to talk to her by phone and say nothing really, just "I love you" and God bless you on your journey. I cried for her death later, but while I was with her I was FOR her. I didn't ask her to comfort me in the loss of my mother; her job as a mother was done a long time before. Her job as a soul in transition was her real job, and it looked like she did a good job of it. A flight of angels really did sing her to her rest.

Note: A friend suggested that I not end the book with this topic. After so much about living a passionate life, to end with death … But what could be more natural? This following exercise might make up for it.

Angels Exercise:

Make a list of everyone in your life who ever gave you encouragement, support, and care. Next to their names write what it was they gave you—spiritual guidance, physical care, monetary support, emotional support, etc.

Take the time to write each of them a letter, thanking them for what they gave you and letting them know what it was; so many "angels" never know they even gave, as it is so much a part of who they are.

Send them the letter and you'll receive "points," but if you really want to accumulate the big pay-off you can add part "b" of this exercise.

In each of the letters that you send, commit either to recreating the support that your angel gave you in someone new or to repaying it; pay it forward or backward. If someone lent you money when you needed it, give it back to him or her. If you've already paid it back and can afford to, give that same amount to a charity or cause in honor of your angel. If it was support along the way as you accomplished something, find a mentoring program or a similar initiative and either give of your time or another resource and tell the story of your angel and what he or she did for you.

Write the letter and send it, even if the person is no longer living. Send it to his or her family or find a way to tell the story of his or her support to encourage others.

Celebrate the heroism of the angels in your life.

Afterword
Transforming the Author

Ten years ago I uncharacteristically missed my then only child's second birthday and in the same week turned down box seats at Chicago's fabulous Lyric Opera. I did this in order to sit with thirty other people on ill-padded chairs in a hotel meeting room for a five-day seminar that would last more than sixty hours. It was the second in a series of three seminars, and despite the uninspiring surroundings I was on fire with new ideas, discoveries, and possibilities. As the seminar leader delivered more of the technology, I was struck with a sense of déjà vu that was literally noticeable; I was in my first level of coursework, but it seemed as if I'd had all of this coaching before.

As the "light bulbs" of discovery continuously went off like cameras on a red carpet runway, I realized that my déjà vu experience was due to the fact that the material of the seminar was nearly exactly the same methodology I used daily in my career at the time as an actor, director, and acting teacher. Nothing the facilitator shared was new—I had a master's degree in it—but it was in a new light, in a parallel application, something I'd never imagined before. It was a mind-blowing experience! I became hooked on personal growth and self-discovery.

Within a year I was the executive director for the training courses I had been a participant in, enrolling others, managing operations, and running the business of the seminars. I retired from a full-time acting and directing job, and on top of my managerial duties I apprenticed under world-class course leaders and began facilitation aspects of the courses from in front of the room and coaching others on an individual basis.

Through the coursework I met a business owner who hired me to eventually be an in-house trainer, but it took me eight years to get the job. I got sidetracked into being the production manager, then general manager as the company grew 500 percent and went from a sketchy regional player to the industry leader. All along I continued my own personal training seminars from several different sources, and I and the other senior managers enrolled so many of our employees into personal growth seminars that we called ourselves a "transformational" company. There was little doubt the application of these "soft" principles made the meteoric rise of our company possible. In fact our application of these contexts and training principles to our specific goals and company vision became a business model of its own: *Making it Happen: No Matter What.*

Through this corporate experience I had over a dozen business and personal coaches over the years, I volunteered as a coach in seminars, and my acting for non-actors course started producing results in other areas of people's lives and morphed into my own unique seminars, "Being the Star of Your Own Life." I've had mentoring as both an executive coach and a personal coach, in due course managing the tenor and topics of our hired coaches and their agendas. I moved from front-line production to full-time in-house consultant, trainer, and performance breakthrough expert—the role I wanted when I first was hired (it only took me eight years to get the job I was hired for). I had transitioned from a stage director to a director in real life, and after two years as chief training officer responsible for coaching, development, and the culture of over one hundred employees, I followed my passion and formed my own firm as a full-time executive and personal coach.

My daily work with people is centered on shining the spotlight on their gifts and talents and helping them, as Marcel Proust said, "see with new eyes." My practice includes start-up business owners, sales professionals, and people unsure of "what's next" but who are committed to living a life of passion, joy, and commitment. It's the best job in the world, and the journey to here has been like thirty years squeezed into ten.

The Hamlet Secret is a compilation of all of the best lessons learned from the many seminars, courses, coaches, and teachers I've worked with personally, whose methodology I've studied and practiced for nearly fifteen years. It contains lessons from theatre, sales training, ontology, and practical application of common sense. It is a personal workshop that will open many doors and create a life of passion, joy, and contentment. Your part in it: "The readiness is all."

Oh yeah, the answer to "To be or not to be": BE, man, BE.

Index